C. C. NIETO-QUINTELA

THE MYTH OF POLITICS

Dialogs of a Professor
with his Students

The Myth of Politics
(Dialogs of a professor with his students)

ISBN-13:9781720468325

Spanish version:

El mito de la política
(Diálogos de un profesor con sus alumnos)

Acknowledgments:

To Eng. Jorge Linares, for his opinions, language suggestions during the preparation of the English version of this book and for our occasional chats about life.

To my sons, branches of this tree and to Chula for sharing with me the waves of the unpredictable sea of life.

CONTENTS

Presentation

After the seminar about the causes of terrorism, now Nick begins a new seminar about politics.

The seminar begins with a brief analysis of the evolution of politics in history, which shows how politics was before the beginnings of our era in primitive communities, the students comment in the class their lecture on the great empires of the antiquity and the seminar continues running until arriving to the XXI Century analyzing how politics evolved through time. In the classes the opinions of several students are taken into consideration as a sample of how politics is seen by general people.

At the end of the seminar Nick shows his certainty about the necessity of the existence of an efficient supranational organism to act as an arbiter among countries and protector of people anywhere in the world, proposal that we already have seen in "Nick", but here he goes beyond and make the first comments on the possibility of the creation of a world community.

What is easy to deduct from the classes of Nick, is his absolute certainty and interest in the value of justice, which at the end means everything that could be desired by people and sufficient for a good coexistence in this world.

Nevertheless this is only the peak of the problem, because coexistence has two ends, on the one side, justice well administered by who are in charge of it, and on the other side the human nature, in his opinion only controllable by the punishment established in the law to offenders, which must be strong enough to discourage people with criminal minds to act against the law.

Understanding the topic

The Myth of Politics

Nick came to the first class of the seminar of Political Theory for graduates announced with the name of *"The Myth of Politics"*, a short seminar with a two months duration in twenty four classes of one hour, three times weekly.

In the class there were several faces he knew from the last seminar: Lora Lord, lawyer; Arnold Man, lawyer; Rag Kumar, philosopher; Sarah Morrison, psychologist; Frederic Mass, economist and Abu Hammad, economist. There were also six new students.

Nick presented himself to the new students and all the students did the same to the class.

The new students were Barbara Larrea, journalist; Emily Kent, Social worker; Philip Shultz, Lawyer; Gregory Robertson, philosopher; Albert Sauer, journalist; and George Lin, engineer.

After the mutual presentation, Nick began the first class.

1

What is Politics?

Today begins this seminar named *The Myth of Politics*. Now that we know each other, I want to make an introduction about this subject that I hope will capture your attention during the next two months. First of all we must have the certainty that everybody understand what Politics is.

Is there anybody who could give us a definition of Politics? He looked around and saw Albert with his arm raised and smiled to him as an invitation to speak.

Albert rose and said: Politics is the science of governing and managing people, to maintain the order and welfare in a country.

Thank you, Nick said and continued.

As of now, I personally reject that politics could be regarded as a science because science means certainty obtained and proved through many tests. Politics is something antagonistic with science, in such a case it could be more appropriated to associate politics with commerce because politicians, he or she, try to sell to the population a political program, announcing and praising its content.

If you ask to several people selected at random about the causes of the problems the world is suffering, you can be sure that in a great percentage the answer would be: Politics. But, is this the real cause? What is your opinion?

The students gave opinions in both senses.

No, Nick said, we cannot blame politics; the real cause of so many situations of disaster that happen in different countries is human nature.

Politics is not the cause but the effect. What needs to be done is a comprehensive study about the human being by its diverse way of thinking, acting and reacting before each situation.

The law exists for that same reason, but not the law itself, but the penalty, the punishment for its violation. For sure everybody knows the content of the fundamental laws because it is in their mind from birth, who does not know that it is wrong to do harm to another?

Humans love pleasure and hate pain and harmful sensations, they know perfectly well that to harm to another is bad, but they do it. Why? Because those people are taken by bad feelings since they are born and that is something to be taken into consideration in politics.

So, we can not say that politicians are bad people, the correct approach would be to say that there are bad politicians, some of them but not all.

It is difficult for a man to know how another man is. A person of ill feelings who wants to deceive and disappoint a fellow being needs to cause a good impression when approaching him, he or she needs to be friendly and likable otherwise it would be difficult for him to deceive. If you apply this to politics you can imagine its practical effect.

The conclusion is that any person can be a general danger, so if one of those persons succeed in achieving to become the ruler of a community, the people of that community will suffer the consequences, for that reason it is so important the existence of elements of control to avoid any excess of a Ruler.

In the Middle Ages, in feudal systems, coexisted the king with the feudal Lords and when a new king had to be elected he should declare under oath the acceptance of his limitations due to the presence and power of the other lords.

To make the king aware of the limitations of his power, the various feudal lords used various forms, this was one of them: "We (the feudal lords) who each one have as much power as you and that altogether have more power than you..." with this statement the king knew that his power was limited by the power of the lords and he had not to exceed the limit of his power.

But I guess you will be asking yourselves, in that case what is politics?

I would say, and do not be surprised, that politics nowadays is something that should not exist because it has become a lucrative activity, a way of living for many people paid by the other citizens, who instead of receiving the just compensation for their contribution through the payment of taxes, they see a worsening of the relations among people as well as the impoverishing of vast sectors of the population.

If we compare the situation of the middle class in any country with the situation they had two hundred years ago, there is no doubt that today people live much better in any sense, in spite of the enormous increase of the world population, because new inventions and the progress in technology makes life easier, and of course people's rights that before were not taken into account now are recognized, nevertheless people are less satisfied, why? Because the majority of the people always want more, no matter what they may have, they want more.

Albert said: If we cannot consider politics as a science, what can we say that is, an art?

No, what kind of art can politics be? Unless you understand by art just an activity.

Politics since the origin of time, has passionate people, but at that time its meaning was different than today, we cannot be in agreement not even with the concepts of great authors, as for example Aristotle, who said that a city is a political association, in my opinion it is not political but social, even to call it association could be arguable. Because in an association it must exist (afectio societatis) that is to say, the will of being in association with the other part, and among the citizens of a community not all are in good relations with the others.

Politics, as I said, always passionate people because it means power and means a better position for politicians with respect to the other citizens, something that should not be.

A happy community is the one where justice works well and everybody has same rights and duties although with different functions.

As I have said on other occasions from this podium, I am here teaching and learning because the exchange of points of view and ideas enriches one's knowledge, for that reason your interventions will be highly appreciated, which I hope will be based on personal investigation and logical deductions.

It is necessary to be cautious and not to be swayed by what you read, whoever the author and the time when it was written. It is necessary to read, analyze under a logic point of view, compare and draw conclusions that should also be taken with caution.

Nevertheless there are great thinkers whose opinions are valid throughout the centuries if we know how to understand and put ourselves into the idiosyncrasy and knowledge of the time when they were issued and we take into account that everybody has good and wrong ideas and among their works someone can be very good whereas others can be mediocre.

Finally I want to posit, which could be an adequate definition for Politics, first from a philosophical point of view, that is to say, from the angle of the "must be" that has nothing to do with the meaning that now has in the political arena.

The purpose of a definition is to explain in a simple and understandable way the meaning of the topic defined. I will avoid etymology mentions that I guess are already well known to any of you, what you have to keep in mind is the subtle difference between politics and policy, this is the established an approved way of doing things not only in politics but in any other organization, so policy could be inside the meaning of politics as for example "the policy of a government about its foreign relations". In English are used at this effect two different words for these two accept-ations: "politics" y "policy".

Politics according with my way of thinking is the activity developed by a State on the one hand using its power to maintain the internal security and the welfare of the citizens and on the other hand, signing and maintaining international treaties and diplomacy to avoid conflicts with other states. To achieve both objectives, is sufficient to consider satisfactory the political activity, nevertheless for several of the most important political philosophers, the only purpose of politics is: "power" and that is the kind of politics that we have to reject because the real purpose must be the welfare of a community of beings.

Such political activity was exercised through several systems many of them not invented for people's benefit but for the personal interest of politicians or political organizations. Some of the principal systems will be the matter of our study, nevertheless in order for you have an idea of the diverse way how politics was used, I'm going to mention just the names of some of the so many political systems that existed in the world: Monarchy, Absolute Monarchy, Parliamentary Monarchy, Democracy, Representative Democracy, Republic, Anarchy, Theocracy, Autocracy, Dictatorship, Communism, Fascism, Socialism, Social Democracy, Capitalism, Technocracy, liberalism and many others scarcely known by people.

Now, based on its current real meaning, we can simply say that Politics is the set of activities developed by one individual or a group of individuals from different trends competing to obtain the management of a State.

Such activities, as are developed nowadays by politicians include several stages in which they will cover: First, to show citizens the advantages of their government program, making possible and impossible offers to the citizens if they win. Second, the dispute with their contenders to whom they seek to discredit using all possible means even slander and lies. Third, the submission to the vote of the citizens who will decide which of the contenders they prefer to rule the country.

Nick saw an arm raised, it was one of the new students named Barbara, a journalist. Nick invited her to talk.

I am curious about the name of this seminar "The Myth of Politics" Why? What does it means?

A good question, answered Nick, in fact I apologize because I had to comment about its meaning.

Why we say that politics is a myth?

Well, to explain that I would have to disclose the content of several further classes, for that reason I prefer to answer your question at the end of the seminar and if it is the case that I forget it, do not hesitate to remind to me,

although then you will have a clear under-
standing about the reason of the name.

Well, we have finished for today, in the next
class we will see how politics appeared in the
world. I like to announce you the matter of
the next class so that you have the opportunity to get some information on the matter,
nevertheless you have the program of the
course where all the contents are included.

2

How Politics appeared in the world

From the moment that for some reason a more or less large group of people met together, to avoid coexistence problems it was necessary to have a ruler capable to take decisions in transcendental moments to the group by setting the direction to be followed or the decision or decisions to be taken to protect the integrity of the group. Those who develop such activity with the passage of the time were called politicians and the activity politics.

I want to remind you that the word Politics comes from the Greek word *polis* that refers to a town usually with walls to protect the city; the inhabitants of the town were the *polytiké.* In the old Athens only men who were born there from an Athenian father were citizens and they could take care of politics. In Rome it was used the same root, "politice" in Latin. The *polytiké* developed the way of governing and the issue of laws and regulations to maintain order, good customs and security for the citizens.

Until that moment politics was an acceptable activity, usually those incipient politicians lent themselves to their homeland a dedication based primarily on his patriotism willing to give their lives for it and rarely for profit.

Does anybody can say how politics appeared in the world?

Emily, moved timidly her hand and Nick pointed her.

As per what it was said, politics appeared as a necessity to maintain the community calm. The people deposited their confidence in someone hoping not to be shortchanged.

What differences do you find with the current politicians? Nick asked.

The student said: In old times politicians developed a personal and altruistic activity in favor of the homeland. Today each political party represents great administrative machinery with a large quantity of people most of them working for a salary, waiting for their party to be the winner to get a reward for their loyalty.

I see that you have understood, Nick said. Now we are going to study how politics in primitive communities was.

* * *

3

Politics in old communities

We commented what politics is and how appeared in the world, now we will pay attention to how politics was in primitive communities, the differences with politics in our days; and afterwards for a better comprehension it is convenient that you know how the great empires in the world were before our era.

I understand that the historic narration in class possibly is not as interesting as a live discussion of a particular topic, but it is as necessary as the experience in people whose retroactive observation is a crucial element of judgment for the future.

We are not going to dedicate these classes to an historic narration by two reasons: first because it would break a little the inter-change of opinions that I consider very im-portant in this seminar and second because with your professional level you must already have a knowledge on the matter, if not in depth at least in a level enough to make a judgment about the facts, nevertheless it was prepared a brief historic summary, he said pointing a bundle of papers that arriving he had put on the table, for those who need to refresh those knowledge and that you can consider an appendixes of the classes of this seminar.

Addressing to Albert that was in the first row said: Would you be so kind to give one to each of your fellow students?

Albert nodded, stood up of his seat, took the papers and distributed them among the assistants.

This historic summary includes: Sumer, Akkad, Babylon, Assyria, Persia, Cartage, Roma, Egypt and China. As is a brief summery of the history of those old empires, you have time to read it and we will dedicate the next class to an interchange of comments about this period of the history of the world.

Even though the historic narration in class, as I have said, could not be as interesting as the live discussion of a particular topic, it is necessary its knowledge as well as the experience in people, whose retrospective observation is a crucial element for the judgment to the future.

I will begin with general and superficial information about politics in the antiquity and after established the subject you will participate with your comments.

If we adopt the term politics to refer to the activity of ruling and establishing order in a community of human beings, there is no doubt that such activity had existed in any sedentary group of people and even in no-madic groups; but, which were the characteristics of that activity in a primitive kinship?

First, it was based on family or group traditions.

Second, the origin of its commands is the Natural Law, or a conscientiousness that everybody has since birth of knowing the distinction between good and bad.

Third, it is a moral code, not a written one, transmitted orally from fathers to sons or from elders to youngsters, logically this makes possible the inaccuracy of the trans-mitted tradition.

Fourth, it has a moral character and is represented by some persons that are kin of the ancestors who gave origin to such tradi-tions.

Fifth, in these systems preserved by tradition, it doesn't exist the law as in State systems, in kinship communities instead of law there are rules of conduct that have passed on from generation to generation.

Sixth, the moral commands in kinship communities are not as compulsory as the law in State systems.

Seventh, the passage of time and the consolidation of Law State Systems affected kinship based communities, avoiding some old customs and rituals not considered civilized any more.

In front of the traditional communities, appeared afterwards whole State systems ruled by the Law, where the law is compulsory not only in a community or a city-state but in the whole territory of the State.

It is with large volumes of population when politics begins to acquire meaning. Then, it appeared as well the complements of the law, as are the judicial systems and punishments established according to the gravity of the offence.

In legal systems the law is written and it is not necessary any more the oral transmission like in kinship systems and of course it is also more secure. A gradual evolution was taking place until our current situation.

Well, Nick said to the class, this is the picture of how what we call politics began to evolve through the times. In my opinion it was decisive the formation of large conglomerates of population in a vast territory under the jurisdiction of a single ruler, proof of this is the existence nowadays around the world of small primitive communities without a legal system which continue being ruled by traditions inherited from their ancestors although they are also subdue by the laws of the State where they are located.

Now, Nick said, I want to know your opinion about those communities ruled by oral traditions inherited from their ancestors. Who is going to begin?

Sarah raised her hand and began: I followed with attention your explanation about old small communities ruled by an oral tradition received from their ancestors, apparently characterized by the absence of laws; nevertheless in the Bible, Exodus 21-1 God says to Moses: *"here are the <u>laws</u> you will give to them"* and punishments by their violation that continue in the numbers 22 and 23, as in a legal system.

I understand your concern, Nick said, but the examples you mentioned do not configure a legal system or have its strength, although have the germ of what with the time would be real legal systems.

Of course in the oldest communities we may remember, there were oral rules, specially prohibitions, imposed by the chief of the community, which if were well accepted survived possibly by generations and were reinforced and even slightly updated by the passage of time. Nevertheless we cannot consider those commands received by tradition as a legal system because they have not its typical characteristics and effects.

The use of the word "law" in the Bible is a simple matter of the terminology used by the transcribers and does not affect its meaning. At first these commands have no name, further they were written and were named laws and when grouped, codes. All the various kinds of laws in a country are what it configured a legal system.

The containing of Exodus 21, 22 and 23, without proceed to analyze its veracity, is a oral transmission that Yahweh makes to Moses of the rules of behavior and punishments for its transgression, then in Exodus 31-18 Yahweh gives to Moses two flagstone written by both sides with the Decalogue of precepts to be accomplished that in Exodus 32-19 Moses break angered seeing his people worshiping a gold bull calf.

Have this clear, the important point is not the container but what it contains, no matter if we call law to something that in fact works as a tradition, it will continue being a tradition in spite of the name we gave to it.

Thank you, I understand the point, Sarah said.

Well, we have arrived to the end of our second class, in the next one, as I have said, we will make a review of the first great empires known in the world, whose history, those who need it, can refresh it with the summary I gave to you.

Please sign at side of your name in the list, for assistance control.

4

The first great empires

For the third class attendance was total; the comments in favor of Nick made by the students that had been in the former seminar were a motivation for others to attend.

Did you make a review of the history of the old empires? Asked Nick

There was a general answer of assent.

Nick began: In our last class we were talking about the meaning of politics, how politics appeared in the world and politics in primitive communities, let us now see how the first great empires of the world were and their characteristics, whose way of functioning mark the political trajectory of subsequent governments in the world and many of their institutions were so well structured that continue being valid in our time, as is the case of several Old Roman legal institutions.

For our purpose, as you had opportunity of seeing, we have considered mainly those empires which appeared before the first century of our era. We will dedicate a short space to this part because it is something about what you can find easily extensive information if you want to go in depth on this matter.

Now, before beginning to comment about those empires, I want to be sure that you have it clear what an empire means. A powerful country governs in a territory but an empire is that country that besides of governing in its own territory governs in several others.

You could appreciate the variable durations of those empires, some of ephemeral duration but not for that less important in their achievements, like was the case of the Macedonian Empire with its capital in Pella, founded by Alexander the Great with a duration of only 11 years (334 BC-323 BC).

There is a geographical area where we can say that appeared the first laws, as if the countries of such area had inquietude to establish regulations to keep the order in their communities. Some of these regulations seem really astonishing for the time when they were issued, but they are not so much because the man was always the same and had same inquietudes and daily problems.

That eagerness to establish laws was repeated in the majority of the countries of that area, some of them profiting from the experience of others. That territory was Mesopotamia, a vast portion of land framed in the Middle East between the Mediterranean Sea and the Persian Gulf throughout the course of the rivers Tigris and Euphrates.

In the territory of Mesopotamia flourished great empires that successively dominated the area, famous were the empires of Sumer, Akkad, Babylon and Assyria.

Is there something in the Sumer civilization that calls your attention taking into account that we are talking of a civilization with more than two thousand years before our era?

Sara said: Theocratic systems were something common in that time, the Assembly of Elders was also normal and in my opinion more effective than the Congress of many countries with immature people still far from having a good knowledge of life. Nevertheless it is interesting the presence of women in the Assembly, which was later on eliminated and only restored recently with the upcoming of democracies.

Nick gave a look to the students waiting for other opinion and it was Frederic who began to talk.

What calls my attention is the verification that the behavior of men was always the same, which means that such behavior is not totally produced by the touch with life but that is something inherent to people since birth. The proof is that more than two millennia before our era they needed legislation on slander, violence and fights among people, as well as to establish punishments for killers, burglars and kidnappers. People used to divorce, commit adultery and acted as false witnesses like now-a-days.

Yes, Nick said, this is the advantage of knowing our past if we want to evaluate our present or our possible future. Is there any comment about the Akkad Empire?

Lora raised her hand asking permission to talk and Nick approved.

It is curious, Lora said, how things repeat themselves in history, I always thought that monarchy so spread in the whole world since the beginning of times has an unavoidable failure: the political transmission by inheritance when nothing warrants the mental capacity of the descendants. The assassination of Sargon sons in Akkad by their own guard never would have happened had they been capable men.

Yes, Nick intervened, that is a situation that was repeated frequently in world history. I guess you will have observed the political and economical instability in all those communities, do any of you desire to comment about its causes?

War, Philip said.

War is a consequence, not a cause, Nick said looking to the others waiting for another answer.

As there was not answer, Nick said: I would say that the causes of instability in those civilizations can be reduced to two causes: first, the rivalry among communities for any reason and second, scarcity of food or other necessary elements. In such circumstances, if a community considered it powerful enough, went on to attack others to get what they needed. As you can see they did not take into consideration justice or any other moral pattern.

So, we see that even though old traditions say that the collapse of the Acadian Empire was due to what it was named "the curse of

Akad", that is to say, a revenge of the gods for the destruction and looting of the E-Kur temple in Nippur, obviously the main cause of the crash was the result of a climate change that produced the crisis that took the country to ruin.

Rag showed that wanted to say something and Nick authorized him.

There is something that I find curious: On the one hand, those old empires were excited with justice and issued the first laws that if we put ourselves for a moment in the shoes of the people of that time, were equitable and inspired in justice; and on the other hand, they invaded other countries and killed people to satisfy their internal needs forgetting justice or any other concept of equity.

What you say, Nick answered, it has been happening along the history of the world and continues happening today.

But that it is not fair, how do you justify that?

Well, Nick said, I don't go to justify, but I can give you an explanation. Countries issue laws because it is absolutely necessary to maintain the internal order, otherwise the country would become chaotic impossible of being governed, to avoid that chaos, the issue of laws generally fair and good for people in general is justified.

The other aspect of invading other territories or to put economic pressure to neighboring countries, it has nothing to do with justice or equity, this obeys to economic needs, imperialist policy, ambition of power or retaliation from previous events.

These arbitrary invasions that always have happened and continue happening can be eliminated only through the existence of a powerful neutral and central world organism with jurisdiction and capacity of action on any State in the world, created to care and maintain the equilibrium of justice in the world, which by now is something improbable for not saying impossible, word that I do not like to use.

Do you have any comment about Babylon?

There was not answer and Nick said: The countries acquire importance and splendor according to who is governing them, Babylon reached its highest splendor under Hammurabi whose code of laws surprised and were admired by future generations.

And do you want to say something about Assyria? There was not answer as well and

Nick asked for Persia. Didn't you find anything relevant?

In general, Abu said, there is not much to
say, all those countries were alike. Perhaps
what deserves a commentary on the Persian
Empire is its internal organization that
reached to all the empire through a good
system of communication, postal service, the
use of a unified language and a strategic
organization of the external dominium to
protect the heart of the empire of external
attacks, possibly would be different if we pay
attention to specific events inside the empire.

Did you find something curious about
Cartage?

Sara raised her hand and Nick authorized her
to talk.

All the Cartage history is an endless war with
its neighbors, I am asking myself, why so
many wars that the only accomplishment was
to weaken the parts in conflict? It seems that
the history of the world is a string of wars in
which people die by hundred or thousands. I
cannot find a justification.

You are right, Nick answered, I think we have
to look for the answer in the human nature,
no mater if a governor is good for his people

40

in his territory, unfortunately people are never satisfied, only when they are in a very bad situation by accepting the suggestions of one of so many demagogues, and remember the old times with nostalgia.

Let us see now the great Roman Empire, I hope it will have called your attention in some way.

Rag raised his hand, Nick approved and he began.

I want to point out something that in my opinion is very important in politics. According to the history, after so many wars that lasted hundred of years, Rome consolidated an empire never exceeded before or after, by any other country in the whole history of the world; then, with the empire came what it was named the "Pax Romana" that lasted for 200 years without wars and this was, in my opinion, perhaps the cause of the fall of the Roman Empire.

Rome, based on its strength, was feared by the other civilizations and could enjoy the comfort of a durable peace at the time that it was losing military strength and the habit of fighting, while its enemies used that time to strengthen themselves and began to attack Rome in several places, with the disadvantage for Rome that now instead of conquering, its task was to defend itself in several places, which produced a tiredness and a wearing off difficult of overcome. In summary: In politics more than necessary, it is essential to be always prepared to face any situation.

It is a good observation, Nick said, only remains Egypt and China to finish our comments on the old empires, let us begin with Egypt, does anybody have a comment?

As at the beginning nobody said anything, Nick said: I would like to call your attention about the political interest represented by the divisions or periods that form the history of Egypt, in my opinion they show how the political power must be renewed of the wear produced by the exercise of the power.

Nick looked to the class and asked: Why?

It must be a bad management of govern, Gregory said.

Philip added: Is the unconsciousness of people who like something but afterwards, no matter how good it could be, they get tired of it.

Emily proposed: I think that the cause is the impossibility of pleasing all people; those in the opposition develop a more important role because while those that are politically satisfied are quiet, the opposition continues bothering all the time making them more notorious.

Sara intervened: in my opinion all what it was said is true, is the human nature.

Well, we have time to deepen in all this in our next classes, Nick said.

Lora wanted to say something and Nick authorized her.

I want to highlight a curious but typical situation along the history of many countries. Egypt had its economy based in agriculture due to the flooding of the Nile River and paradoxically the lowest class of the population, except the slaves, was that of the farmers that cared for the agriculture. That does not sound fair at all!

If you use a magnifying glass to evaluate the economy of the majority of the countries, Nick answered, you will find many similar cases.

All right, Nick continued, we will dedicate our last comments to China, a very interesting old civilization whose analysis will permit to make a comparison with those others of Occident and Middle East.

I would like to know your comments about the role the China policy has represented in the world, and a comparison with the Occidental empires, which are the peculiar characteristics of the China policy and in general any observation you want to make. Nick finished and gave a look to the students.

You George, do you have any observation?

Not one, several, George said, I find very interesting the China civilization, I have traveled to China recently and I have to say that I was favorably impressed by its recent evolution that puts China at the level of the first countries of the world

We are talking about politics, Nick said, what do you like? Do you like the communist system?

Absolutely not, even more, after finishing my studies of engineering I traveled to Russia in the last few years of the Soviet Union with the curiosity of seeing how it was and then there I remembered the "Animal Farm" of George Orwell.

I do not want to be critical, so I will limit myself to say that I didn't see happy people but resigned people in poverty without hope, while a few politicians were powerful as we could to see them at the fall of the system to spread them all over the world with great fortunes.

Now, to answer your question about what did I like of China, I will say that is a political organization that really functions, what is difficult to find in any country worn away by the rivalry of the political parties, not interested in their homeland but in their personal or party interest.

Do you think that the Chinese policy is more effective? Nick asked.

Look at the results; while other countries wear them off in political fights, China in a few years has projected itself as an international power.

What is your opinion? Nick asked to the class.

Rag wanted to intervene and said: everything in life has a price, if we receive something we must pay something. The progress of China is undeniable, but the price that their people have to pay is liberty.

That's all right, Nick said, that is a good point of view that takes us to a brief analysis about the meaning of civil liberty. I want to hear an opinion.

Lora Lord intervened: I don't know exactly the level of freedom that the Chinese people has, but I know that they are traveling around the world establishing business to sell goods imported from China and investigating new business abroad to establish them in China. That class of activity has nothing to do with the typical situation of communist countries where people have problems to move around.

Then about this, my question is: What is the freedom a person has to have?

Freedom has no limit, you are totally free or you are not free, Albert said.

Hearing this, Sara Morrison said: Excuse me, but if I do not remember badly you are a journalist.

Yes, that's correct, Albert answered.

That it is not personal, but in my opinion thinking in that way I'm afraid that your communication with the public cannot be adequate because you will be inviting them to act according to their will forgetting any rule.

What do you mean? Albert asked.

I mean that you are wrong if you are thinking that the freedom of a citizen is to do whatever he wants. This is the cause of the majority of the disorders that are happening in many countries, where people do no accept limits to their will.

Nick interrupted, it's enough, you are changing an exchange of opinions into a discussion.

What I want to say, Sara continued, is that liberty is not something that people decide but the law, and each one is free only inside the frame of the law and the destiny of those that overpass its limit is the chaos.

You are right, Nick said, and addressing to the class: I would like to know your opinion about the role of China in the history of the world.

Philip stood up and began: as a lawyer I am more familiar with the Roman legacy but by professional curiosity and to make compare-sons I have investigated the legal system of other legislations as the Islam, China,

German and Anglo-Saxon countries and my conclusion is that the combination of the Roman Law was never matched in the history of the world. With respect to China, it established legal regulations since at least one millennium BC but in a different way than occidental countries, China mixed the legal dispositions with the traditions of Confucianism in its legal system.

A relevant difference between the old China and Occident is the procedure in cases of criminal jurisdiction In traditional China it was the own judge who made the investigation of the crime to adopt a fair decision, considering that the assistant of the parts were there looking for a material benefit in detriment of the parts.

It does not seem the Chinese system could have influenced the occidental legal systems for two reasons: first, by the lack of contact during many centuries between Orient and Occident, except for some commercial relations, and second by the great difference between the occidental systems and the Chinese system ruled in great part by moral rules of behavior proceeding from the philosophy of Confucius.

Nick addressed a glance to the students looking for some one that wanted to intervene

but there was no answer and said: in our
next class we will examine the contraposition
between politics and religion to continue
afterwards with the famous event that shook
the world: the French Revolution.

5

Politics and Religion

After greeting the students Nick began:

I imagine that you will be thinking about what is the reason for a religion class in a politics seminar.

Politics and religion were always together, as a symbiosis mutually useful to each other.

Religion existed in the world since man exists and prior to any written records of its presence on earth, first attempting to give explanation to natural phenomena associating them with people behavior. If you receive something bad is because you behaved badly or have done something forbidden in the community.

Some questions that can arise are:

Why religion is present in some way in every community of people in the world? It was the response to a necessity to reassure people who was terrified by natural phenomena, illness and death, for which they had no explanation.

It is enough to imagine a man in a primitive community walking at night in a forest, in the middle of an electric storm, receiving the impact of hailstones, seeing the effects of an earthquake or any other natural phenomenon still without explanation to him.

The remains found in the oldest graves as in Atapuerca (Spain), Pontnewydd (Wales), Krapina (Croatia) were considered rites of religious inspiration, though nothing supports that, and they could also be a simple manifestation of the pain that a human being feels by the loss of a family member or a companion.

In spite of the several theories that do their best to find a divine origin to religions, the origin of so many religions is only human, by the simple fact of being so many, is as if people have gods *a la carte.* Most people have the religion that their parents had.

Why each religion is different to the others? Because each religion was managed by different men, of different geographic location and worried by different things, nevertheless it was common that religions were copied from former religions, sometimes even using the same gods. This can be seen even in the main religions, we find in Christianity teachings of

Judaism and in Islam those of Christianity and Judaism.

Which is the degree of credibility of a religion? None, nothing that they say can be verified, proved or backed by the reason or the logic.

If nothing supports religion's teachings, why have they survived through the time? They have survived by fear and ignorance. By fear mainly to illness and death or even to the power of the own religion and, with respect to ignorance, it is not ignorance of knowledge but of how to reason.

Everybody has the capability of using his mind to distinguish between goodness and badness or between good and evil, but such capability is scarcely used and people prefer to be guided by their senses or by the words of somebody who makes them impossible promises that could never be verified or could be accomplished.

Unfortunately that kind of people is the majority in any country, they are deceived again and again even by the same person, but they never learn, both in religion and in politics.

Why polytheism derived in monotheism? At the beginning it was by the necessity of offering something new, besides, it was easier to present the image of one God instead of many gods. Additionally the commands of an only God are stronger and not discussed by other gods as we could see frequently in narrations of the pantheon of the old Greek religion.

Which is the reason of the symbiosis between religion and politics? It is a pragmatic reason, they need each other. This was more relevant in other times than now, when religions are losing force to the extent that the majority of people are having more access to knowledge and are less ignorant.

In fact, in my opinion, religion should be completely separated from politics to avoid possible mutual disastrous influence.

In general to practice a religion it is not bad, except if the religion promotes actions that are against the natural law, even more the processions or other rituals in some religions became traditions and are an amusement for the population, but what is absolutely important is that politics is not affected by religion.

What religion has to be accepted in a country? All of them *can* be accepted, but without external manifestations, no processions, bell strokes, calls to prayer or any other external manifestation that could be unpleasant for other people. Regarding temples, they must be accepted only on a reciprocal basis.

Any question about this relation between Politics and Religion?

There is something that some time ago caught my attention, Albert said, I was born in a Christian family and I read and heard many times about the monotheistic character of this religion but I never saw so many images (any way idols) in any other religion.

Nick made a gesture with his hands to stop the comment and said: Your comment is not relevant to our class; we are not analyzing the particulars of the religion, but the relations between politics and religion, any religion.

I'm sorry, Albert apologize.

Is there somebody else? Nick asked.

There was not response and Nick proceeded to begin a new topic.

* * *

6

The French Revolution

The French Revolution of 1789, Nick began, can be considered as a departure point to a new order of things in the world, it is not our purpose to analyze here in depth this revolutionary process but to highlight its effect in politics, not only in France but in the whole world, otherwise we would need a whole seminar only for this matter.

Even though people in France succeeded in overthrowing the monarchy and establishing a republic in 1792, the new republican period was unstable and violent, nobody was safe and the Guillotine had permanent work during the almost ten years of the revolution.

Can any of you say to us what has represented the French Revolution to the politics of the world?

Lora Lord raised her hand and said: in my opinion this revolutionary process opened the mind of the mass of people to the possibility of intervene actively in politics. People was aware of the strength of the multitude when

is decided to change things or die and they
have the bravery of doing it. Of course, there
are several factors that can accelerate, slow
down or fail the project, as the quality of the
ruler, to have at least some knowledge of
strategic, an important number of followers,
etc.

Your point of view is correct, Nick said and
continue, effectively after the French Revolution we always find in any country two parts
well defined: governors and governed, but
now linked by a tacit contract: The Social
Contract, many times materialized in a physical instrument: a Constitution.

We can find rudiments of this recognition of
rights in former Letters of Rights "Bill of
Rights" although they had a different character because instead of a contractual touch
they were better a concession of the ruler
obliged by the circumstances. The social
contract puts both parts joined in a situation
where each one must accomplish its part,
though in practices the reality could be different.

If the mass of people, the governed, feel
themselves oppressed or defrauded by the
governor in the accomplishment of his
obligations and decide to break the contract
through civil disobedience and stop the

functioning of the country, they couldn't fail. Do you agree?

At first yes, Frederic said.

What does "at first" mean? Nick asked.

In my humble opinion that it is not so simple, Frederic argued, we have to take into account that the government has the army and all other organisms and tools to maintain the order, which can use against its opponents, while the people is defenseless, consequently it is not so clear the victory of the citizens.

We have at this moment a typical example of this situation in a South American country, Venezuela, where the human rights of people do not exist and the population is defenseless against all kind of abuses of gangs of motor-cyclists supposedly armed by the government who commit daily robberies, abuses and deaths to the citizens who don't know what to do and are imprisoned simply by expressing their opinion and protest against the general scarcity of food and pharmaceutical products, a very rich country where now people is suf-fering hunger thank to a corrupt government that kidnapped the country and destroyed until misery one of the richer countries of South America. What is the utility of the Social Contract for them?

You are right, Nick approved, but the behavior of the government it will be observed and judged by the other countries.

Excuse me professor, Frederic interrupted, neither the other countries nor the international community will do anything, remember other Caribbean country, Cuba, is supporting political and social abuse for more than 60 years. Who has done something for that country? Venezuelans and Cubans in their defenselessness, escape to other countries if they have the possibility, even those in worse economic situation also escaped and continue escaping risking their lives to go where they are accepted. In my opinion the international policy is a great business.

I understand what you say and your concern that I know that is true, but you have to recognize that the own citizens of these countries and of other countries in similar situations must assume their part of guilt, you know how the governments of these two countries arrived to the power, in Cuba through a revolution supported by the population and in Venezuela through free elections in which the population voted for a new government that finally took them to this.

It is possible that at the beginning the people could be blinded by the usual false promises, but soon the quality of the government is notorious and is the moment of doing something, nevertheless as you said, those of better economic level preferred to abandon the country to wait abroad the fall of the government that contrarily was taking control of all the important organisms and institutions included the army and in some years it was too late for an easy solution, this is more the case of Venezuela, because in Cuba from the beginning the revolutionary killed anybody who did not agree with them terrifying the population and besides with the support of Russia tried to export Communism to other countries and succeeded with Venezuela, which became its political satellite and source of income.

Bad governments rarely can be defeated from abroad, it is necessary to be in the country and defend it, I do not see that in your examples, contrarily people abandon and go to other country to wait the oppressor government fall by itself, which rarely will happen.

It is absolutely necessary the intervention of all citizens or at least of a majority of them and the firm decision of restoring the rights of the population and do not go backwards in their determination under no concept.

Any way I understand the concern of living in a country where to survive is like a lottery preoccupation that, I understand, people feel more for their family than for them, knowing that the authorities that are supposed to protect you instead of doing it ignore the situation and favor insecurity and crime.

Well, we are out of our topic of today, let us return again to the famous revolution, Nick said.

Although the population of France succeeded in overthrowing the monarchy and establishing a republic in 1792, the new republican period was unstable and violent, nobody was safe and the guillotine had permanent work during the almost ten years that lasted the revolution.

The outcome was the Napoleon's dictatorship, but the seed of the French Revolution with its radical ideas was spread by the wind, produced the fall of other monarchies and was also the inspiration for the independence of most American colonies.

In your opinion, why was the French Revolution produced? Nick said waiting an answer from the students.

By the oppression of the monarchy, Colin said.

I think that there were several factors acting together to produce such a violent turmoil of the multitude. Frederic added.

Effectively, Nick began, the factors were several, the continuous wars in Europe produced erosion in all countries to the point almost of bankruptcy, which the government attempted to solve with more taxes on the population already very much oppressed and suffering at that moment several bad harvests.

Nevertheless, perhaps the spark that lit the wick was the contrast between the poverty of people and the great opulence and privileges of the aristocracy and clergy that considered themselves as a different kind of people than those who worked in the country or in other crafts. This reminds us the comment of Lora when we were talking about Egypt.

After the famous assault on the Bastille, it was issued the *Declaration of the rights of man and of the citizen* and immediately were abolished all the privileges the old regime had granted to the highest classes.

The resolution of the Third State and its invitation to the others to participate was made without considering whether they had or not the support of other states. The declaration as National People's Assembly, their decision to rule the national business and to give France a constitution, which was confirmed in an oath taken at the real tennis court on June of 1789, produced its effect.

Soon the Assembly began to receive the support, curiously first, from those whom they wanted to destroy, so they got the adhesion of most of clergy representatives and many aristocrats perhaps not thinking if the movement was right or wrong but in its strength and in their own protection siding themselves with the stronger side. Messages of support arrived from all France.

Apart from Paris, the representatives of the government in provinces acted out of control abusing and killing without justification or by their own convenience in a great sample of injustice and corruption.

Liberal reforms came one after the other: divorce, abolition of race discrimination related to black people and Jews, abolition of slavery in French colonies, abolition of feudalism, free choice of religion and many others, but at the same time those were insecure times where anyone could be accused of having traditional ideas or of being an aristocrat or collaborator, which was enough to send him to the guillotine. And thus the king and the queen were also executed as well as all those aristocrats who did not have the opportunity to abandon the country.

This atmosphere of insecurity affected not only the upper classes but also the revolutionaries themselves, their rulers and governments changed fast, moved by the extremely radical attitude of the people who made thousands of individuals (around 40,000) to be judged by revolutionary courts and immediately executed.

The French Revolution through different periods of government, Jacobins, regime of Terror, Termidorian, and the Directory ended with the Consulate, established by Napoleon Bonaparte, through a Coup of State after his successful military campaigns abroad that began in 1792, where his army charged against the enemy with a revolutionary fervor comparable to the religious fervor that took Islam in the seventh Century to their conquests in Southern Europe and the North of Africa.

Now the motivation was represented by three magic words: *Freedom, equality, fraternity*

(<u>Liberté, égalité, fraternité</u>) and also for a song that became a symbol for ever in France "La Marseillaise"

Napoleon Bonaparte (born in Corsica in August 15, 1769) intervened in more than 55 battles placing France at the summit of the world.

His activity was not limited to the military field; in 1804 he introduced in France a Civil Code (for ever known as Napoleon Code) that inspired further legislation in other countries.

The Senate proclaimed Napoleon Emperor and on December 2nd, 1804 at the cathedral of Notre Dame in Paris during a ceremony in presence of the Pope, Napoleon crowned himself.

But fortune is unstable and in 1814 in the Treaty of Fontainebleau, Napoleon had to accept his exile at the Island of Elba.

On February 20, 1815 Napoleon escaped from Elba and arrived to Paris on March 20, beginning what were named the Hundred Days of Napoleon, but the die was cast and after the Battle of Waterloo, the government of Louis XVIII was restored on June 28, later on October 16th Napoleon is exiled in <u>Saint</u>

<u>Helena</u> a small island in the South Atlantic where he died on May 5th, 1821.

The incidents and events of the French Revolution are matter of reflection; in them we can see the effect of the human nature and consequently events that repeated before and after, while others are the result of the firm resolution of people addressed to a specific purpose. We can see also how uncontrollable, pitiless and terrible can be the multitude when is left to their own criteria.

In its several phases, the French Revolution killed not only the aristocracy and clergy but also civil people and to their own revolutionary, because the governors of today, could go tomorrow in the "tumbrel" to the guillotine.

7

Colonialism
Independence movements

When Nick came into the classroom the murmurs of voices of the students stopped as they prepared to pay attention.

Last class, Nick began; we commented a transcendental event in the history of the world, the French Revolution, if I say transcendental, is because many of the subsequent stages in the history of the world were affected in some way by this revolutionary movement.

Today we are going to talk about colonialism and the independence movements in America. I would like to know what colonialism means to you. Is there any volunteer who can tell us what he understands by colonialism?

Sarah Morrison raised her hand and began: Colonialism occurs when a state invades another state and submits it to its political system and its administration.

Without coming into other explanations about its origin, what Sarah says is correct, Nick said. Is there any other opinion?

About the origin of colonialism, Frederic said, I think it corresponds to modern history because in old history there were vast empty territories that were invaded and populated by the invader and if some inhabitants were found they were subdued or enslaved, in my opinion it was something different, this is what I would call colonization. To me colonialism must begin with an invasion and the subdue of other territory organized in any way as a country, with its own rules and administration and being forced to accept the laws and administration of the invader, besides nowadays there is not free territories.

Effectively, Nick said, colonialism properly said began as a result of the discovery and conquest of the American territories in the XV Century. Spain, England, France and Portugal divided among them the new territories, but new territories where there were other cultures that were subdued by the use of more powerful weapons; the existing cultures were substituted by those of the conquerors.

Before moving on to another question we have to specify something with respect to the colonialism in America. We have talked of colonialism in a generic way, but it is convenient that you have a clear view of its shapes.

When we speak about colonialism we are not talking of the start of an activity but of its result, that is to say, about a territory controlled from the State of other territory more or less remote.

But, how is the beginning of that activity that produces the existence of a colony? That will depend of the circumstances found by the invaders, if in that place already exists a civilization able of containing them and with a higher strength, there will be no invasion and, of course, no colonialism, but commerce interchange, if there are products or raw materials of interest, as it was done by the old Phoenicians in all the Mediterranean Sea or the commercial expeditions between Occident and the Chinese Empire.

If the invaders find an organized civilization that can likely be defeated, then the conquest will happen to dispose of their products or raw materials, such was the case in Central and South America that became later on colonial territories. Although at that moment that concept was not used, because the new territories passed to be part of the invader state, which pretended govern them from its territory through public representatives designed ad hoc.

There are people that distinguish the conquest of Central and South America from that of North America. Considering that the last one was not conquest but colonization, opinion that I do not share by the following:

It is true that in the first expeditions arrived from Spain, except those that directed them were integrated by individuals of a very low level, because it was not easy to find people willing to enroll in such an adventure, due to the popular, and even not popular, belief that the Atlantic Ocean could finish in bottomless abysses.

After the first trip and motivated by the news spread by the sailors about the existence of enormous wealth in those lands, there were many who wanted to go to the new world, but any way no so much as it could believe, proof of this is that after the Toledo Agreement of July 26th 1529, and in accordance with what it was established in it, Francisco Pizarro must set sail to America in a term of six months taking with him 150 men that he could not get and had to set sail evading the inspection of the authorities.

Those who consider that the colonization of North America was better because it was made up of families pursued by religious beliefs, they forget that in North America there was about 90 different ethnic groups with an approximated total of 10 million Indians of several characteristics, that those English Puritans and those who came after them were exterminating as almost did among themselves in their religious fanaticism, that compelled many of them to run away to other places. Without taking into account that all the South of the actual United States was also Spanish territory.

A trip made at the beginning of the XX Century by the three Americas, would show to any observer the reality of the result of both kinds of colonization, for me both disastrous, but while in South America we can see to prevail in the population a miscegenation of whites, Indians and blacks, in North America there would be an almost totality of net European and black features. What happened with the 10 million Indians that there were before the European occupation?

Then, the only reason that I find to say that in North America there was colonization is the fact that they named the groups of people arrived "colonies", remember the 13 States that were named the 13 colonies.

It was said also that the Spaniards came to America to sack the gold, what did the English, French and even the Dutch do? To loot the same gold but from the Spanish ships, evidently piracy was much easier and productive than the search and extraction in the inland.

I think that this is enough; do you have any observation on this respect?

Albert raised his hand and said: All this is very controversial and I agree with you in saying that all the occupation in America, any of them, was disastrous. Regarding the looters, all of them were in one or another way, and those that were not it was because they had not the opportunity, it's enough to remember when in later times gold was discovered in California and how things were, or the presence of Englishmen and Portuguese in China and Southeast of Asia.

In summary, of what I am convinced is about how correct was Plauto already in the times of the old Rome when he said: "homo hominis lupus est" that is to say, the man is a wolf for the man.

With respect to your last observation, Nick said, I find more correct the position of Thomas Hobbes saying: "Man is a kind of God for man; and man is an errand wolf for man" affirming that definitions are correct, that is to say, in the human race there are good and bad people, unfortunately the last ones are the more abundant.

Tell me now ¿what is your opinion about the invasion of the American Continent? Nick asked to the class.

Several hands were raised and Nick pointed to Rag Kumar.

I believe that it is difficult to give an appropriate opinion considering the distance in time, it is always necessary to take into account the moment when this occurred, and at that time wars among countries and invasions were a daily activity, if we add up the fact that the discoverers found in the new world abundant wealth, that is enough to move people.

If the access to the new world would not have been limited by the characteristics of the transport available at the time, Europe would have moved entirely to America. This is not something of that time; today it would be even worse if a discovery like that could be possible.

I agree with you, Nick said. Now I would like to know your opinion about how the process was developed by the conquering countries.

Now it was Lora Lord who raised her hand and began to say: The process of conquest or colonization if you want, was different according with the countries, of course Spain as it was the first to arrive had some advantage, soon Portugal began to discus the right on the new lands to the point that only less than two years after the discovery, in June 1494 it was celebrated the Treaty of Tordesillas signed in Tordesillas (Castile, Spain) and ratified in Setubal (Portugal), by which the lands discovered outside of Europe would be divided between Spain (Castile and Leon) and Portugal in the following way: taking as reference a line or meridian at 370 leagues west of Cape Verde Islands, the lands that could be discovered to the East of that line would belong to Portugal and the lands to the West of the line to Spain, At first the treaty that was approved by the Pope worked well, but soon, as all the other countries in Europe had been ignored, they ignored the treaty, specially the Protestant countries that rejected a decision of the Pope.

England and also, in a lower proportion, France focused on the more lucrative and less laborious activity of piracy, raiding and looting ships that came from America.

About the development of the process of colonization it was different in each country. In Spain the Crown considered according with the information received by the explorers that the people they found were primitive and naïve like children and the kings ordered the elaboration of a whole system of laws adequate to them that was named Right of Indies, which was softer than the one used in Spain, unfortunately the representatives of the Castile Crown taking advantage of the distance from Spain did whatever they wanted in detriment and even with great abuse of the natives, up to the point that it seems that there was a kind of proverb among the Spanish rulers in America regarding the orders and laws that came from Spain that said: "The laws are obeyed but not applied"

Occasionally those abuses were discovered and denounced and corrupts punished and removed, most of the time to be substituted by others who possibly did the same.

Perhaps the worse role was represented by the Church that obliged people to convert to the Christian faith without any choice, they could even torture or kill the reluctant.

It is well known the protests of the Spaniard Fray Bartholomew de las Casas against the Indian slavery during his life and in his book "A short Account of the Destruction of the Indies" He was in America first appointed as "Protector of the Indies" Any way he couldn't do much against the colonizers and passed to the history as the creator of the "Black legend" of Spain in its colonization.

But what was much more serious was the destruction that the church made of the documents and the background of those civilizations that were burned or destroyed describing them as heresy.

Summarizing we can say that the policy could be good but its application bad.

The government of Spain in Central and South America began to deteriorate promoted not by the lower levels of the population in the colonies, but by the highest stamens, that is to say, by the Spaniards and descendants that got rich through the concessions of the crown and their own abuse on the native communities, ignoring the Spanish Right of

Indies that had been created specially for American territories.

Over time the high class in America was tired of paying taxes to Spain, at the same time that they were proud of being Spaniards because they had not other better choice at the time.

The perfect moment arrived when Spain, weakened by the Napoleonic wars, was unable to pay enough attention to the problems of its territories in America. When Ferdinand VII was taken to France by Napoleon, the promoters of the separation from Spain alleging to defend the rights of Ferdinand VII began the first movements of independence from a Spain that had become French and supposedly in defense of Ferdinand VII rights.

Really what they were defending were their own interests. The creation of the *"Supreme Central and Governmental Junta of Spain and the Indies"* in 1808 solved momentarily the problems about the administration of other territories in America and Asia establishing a representation of all councils in Spain and also of the viceroyalties of New Spain, Peru, New Granada and Buenos Aires; the general captaincies of Cuba, Puerto Rico Guatemala and Chile; Venezuela and Philippines.

The fall of the Spanish forces and the French dominium in Spain promoted the apparition of several Councils in America of ephemeral life, the first ones were in Chuquisaca and Quito followed by several others after the reverse suffered by the Spanish forces in the Battle of Ocaña.

The leaders who favored the independence instead of showing their purpose, masked their real intention by saying that they were defending the rights of Ferdinand VII to prepare the population for the final outcome. So in 1824 after more than a decade of wars all American territories were independent from Spain who only maintained Cuba, Puerto Rico and Philippines.

Portugal at the moment of the discoveries was an important power on the sea. Before Columbus arrived to America it seems that already in 1473 the Portuguese arrived to the area of Greenland and Labrador that they named "Newfoundland of the codfish". There are documents that testify the further presence of Portugal in the United States and later in the south, especially in Brazil.

The Portuguese colonization after several explorations was concentrated in the area of Brazil, it began with the European disembarkation in 1500 of its discoverer, Pedro Álvares Cabral and continued until their independence in 1822.

Portugal had to overcome and expel French and Dutch settlers that had settled down in several places of the territory that belonged to Portugal, like Rio de Janeiro, Recife, areas of Paraiba, Pernanbuco and others, what was achieved in 1530

The king of Portugal divided the territory of Brazil in large spaces (Captaincies) that were distributed among the Portuguese nobility for life and in a hereditary way, which permitted to the crown of Portugal to receive income and to reduce the expenses of colonial maintenance to the minimum possible, because the nobles licensee had to cover all the expenses of the colonization, as well as the preaching of the Gospel to the indigenous population.

Nevertheless, in 1549 the king centralized the administration of Brazil designing a Major Captain to represent him and followed the advice of the ultramarine Council. This measure of the king of Portugal was of uncertain utility because the General Captains continued acting at their will keeping all their privileges and even slaving Indians that, to capture them organized expeditions (bandeiras) that with such a purpose went to the Amazon wilderness to look for them, the shortage of captures of native slaves moved the Portuguese settler to bring African slaves.

Portugal received from Brazil products such as gold and diamonds, coffee, sugar cane, dyes, rubber and several others of great commercial interest.

Portugal developed an activity similar to that of the old Phoenicians establishing commercial points spread in this case by the world. Apart of Brazil, Portugal established commerce establishments in Macao, Nagasaki, Bahrain, Bombay, Goa, Ceilan, Moluca islands, India, Oman, Indonesia, China and many other places.

England and France that had preferred to look for a more profitable practice to the discovery of America, restricting them to collect the fruits of the effort of the Spaniards intercepting their ships and stealing their load. As far as colonization was concerned,

England addressed its activity to the North of America in competition with the French that had occupied part of the North East of the present United States and part of the South East of the present Canada. On their side, the Spaniards had in what is today the United States: Texas, Nuevo Mexico, California, Alabama, Mississippi, Oregon, Washington and Florida, where in 1565, Pedro Menendez de Aviles founded San Agustin, the oldest city founded by Europeans in the United States only exceeded in years by San Juan of Puerto Rico

English colonization began with an assignment made by Elizabeth I of England to the pirate Walter Raleigh to whom by his great feats of piracy in favor of the crown, had received the title of "Sir", consisting in founding a colony to the East of North America that was named Virginia and occupied great part of the East coast of the present United States, except Florida that was occupied by the Spaniards.

Soon large crops of tobacco were established, financed the first of them in London by the Company of Virginia, and in 1607 a group of English colonizers arrived and settled in Virginia where they founded a small city (Jamestown) that grew up with an economy based on the farming of tobacco, of which they sent to England the first load in 1614

In New England, on the North East coast of the United States, English puritans besieged by religious problems began to arrive and established several colonies, of which is known the one established in Plymouth in 1620 by the pilgrims who arrived in the "Mayflower". Nevertheless the puritan colonizers arrived running away from the religious intolerance, that they adopt it themselves in America making that a part of them had to emigrate to Connecticut, escaping from an insufferable religious fanaticism that considered that the government had to impose the moral of God and only permitted to vote those registered in the church whose priests were paid with the money of taxes.

A puritan, Roger Williams, who had an opinion on the contrary and said that politics and religion had to be separated, was expelled from Massachusetts in 1635, and then he founded another colony in Rhode Island where he promoted freedom of religion and the separation of religion and State. Several other colonies were founded later on in the same area where religion's freedom was respected.

In 1733 the known 13 English colonies that occupied the Atlantic coast of the present United States from New Hampshire, including Georgia, were already well defined.

Several confrontations on the one hand with the French in the North East of North America and on the other hand, with the English government by the continuous taxes, led in 1775 to the beginning of the war between the 13 colonies and England, being this struggle won due to the help given to the supporters of independence by Spain and France.

In the Versailles Treaty of 1783, England had to recognize the independence of the 13 colonies that these had already established in 1776 in the Declaration of Independence of the United States.

In 1787 the Constitution was approved and in the elections that followed George Washington was elected as the first President of the United States.

* * *

The French colonization began later, in the XVII Century with the founding of Quebec (present Canada) in 1608 by Samuel

Champlain. Its main activity was skins' commerce with the natives.

Quebec was followed by Montreal and several other places, without great importance, in the Great Lakes region. A century later there was a French presence in the area of Niagara, Detroit, Illinois and in the South in New Orleans, which shows a different kind of colonization with respect to the English one that spread along the coast while the French did it inland.

Apart from their centers in North America, the French also opened several centers in the Caribbean area: Saint Dominique (Haiti) San Martin, Saint Croix, San Bartholomew, Saint Christopher y Grenada are some of them, where the French employed black slave labor.

In the XVII Century Louis XIV centralized the administration of the colonies designating Canada as a French province under the command of a general governor, applying the same system of administration to the other colonies.

In 1803 Napoleon sold Louisiana to the United Estates by fifteen million dollars, an important amount for that time as it was enormous the extension of territory negotiated.

* * *

In general, the American decolonization was produced in an interval that we can frame it since the first confabulations until the end of the majority of the conflicts, between the years of 1765 and 1826.

We have finished our comments about this process, now you may begin the comments you deem appropriate.

There was a moment of silence while the students were remembering what had been said.

George Lin raised the hand and began: There are so many aspects to take into consideration in the colonization of each country that what would be more advisable is to choose those common to all of them.

We can analyze, for example, the motivation of each colonizer and in my opinion at the beginning; there was not such intention, but only a commercial purpose.

The Spaniards made their first trip looking for a better route for the spices' commerce. The Portuguese, even before Columbus, were motivated by fishing, especially that of the cod fish, and the first motivation of French was the fur's trade, which had in Europe a great market; the circumstances and the wealth they found changed the original intention making advisable to the countries to extend their domination to the new discovered lands, what also seemed very easily accessible by the superiority of the military power of the invaders.

Also it deserves to be analyzed from a humanitarian angle, the acting of each colonizing country with respect to the indigenous population they found in America, and here we have to consider two positions: that of the respective metropolis on the one side, and on the other side, that of the representatives in America of those countries.

It could be said that referring to the colonizing countries we see in Spain a concern for the natives that is materialized in the creation of a body of laws (Laws of the Indies) that pretends to protect them, concern we do not see in the other countries although the effort of the crown of Castile at that time did not produce much result in the hands of governors that do their will.

On the other hand, if we examine the behavior of the representatives of each country with the indigenous population, the more pitiless seems to have been that of Portuguese, followed by the French, English and after the Spaniards, although none of them deserves an approval.

Talking in general, what is missing, George continued, is that none who has in his mind the sense of justice can approve any process of conquest and colonization.

Any comment of someone else? Nick asked.

I believe, Arnold Man said, that we have to consider relevant the bad intervention of the church, or better of the churches, I do not approve any kind of evangelization, I believe that each one has the right to decide by himself, it is not fair to try to achieve followers by convincing them with the help of dubious purpose and much less by the strength and coercion.

You are right, Nick said, we have finished for today.

8

Political Systems

We can call "political system" the way how a nation or a plural group of nations are ruled under the power of a State in a specific territory. For our purpose we are not interested now in imperialist or colonialist movements, because they are a specific political behavior of any political system, that is to say, are a consequence of them.

As we have seen in our former comments the traditional way of government around the world was reduced first to kingdom systems and after to monarchy, republic, dictatorship and also tyranny, of all of them we can find abundant examples in the history of the world.

In those traditional times, the ruler was not elected by the voters but from inheritance or from a popular or military acclamation.

It is not necessary to say that today or yesterday the result of a new government is like a lottery, depending on several circumstances as: the real character of the ruler and his/her aptitude, change of behavior of the ruler influenced by power, the fairness of his/her decisions and the behavior of those representing the several sectors of the government.

There are other factors that also influence the result of a government independently of the governor, as are the economic circumstances that could affect the welfare of the population, for example a mainly farming country suffering several years of bad harvests or an economic siege of other countries difficult to overcome.

Other important factor that has to be considered is the characteristics of the population, their customs and traditions that have to be taken into account by the ruler, and if they are an obstacle to the fairness of justice or of a good governance, the governor should need to solve the problem but he will have to make a good analysis prior to any law that is going against the tradition.

Important changes in the structure of political systems happen only caused by great changes in the structure of the world, as in the case of the industrial revolution that changed the internal functioning of the countries, as they were adopting the new ways of production, originating the necessity of political adjustments or even new kinds of political systems pushed by the demands of the workers.

After the industrial revolution the exodus from the country to the cities was permanent as an attempt of the workers to survive, which preferred to change a situation of suffering almost without any hope subdued to climate changes for a new one with a secure salary regardless of the efforts they had to do.

We can have an idea of what life was like for the peasants in the country, to accept the exploitation to which they were subjected in the early days at the factories of the big cities.

Nevertheless as always happens, the excessive demands of the employers produced a logic reaction: the union of the workers using the only instrument that they found effective: the strike.

Soon the workers learned that acting separately they were nothing, but together they were a power. This is a productive truth that people should keep always in mind.

That is how a new power emerged in the world: the Trade Unions, which although they were intended to protect workers, they often protected more and first to their own representatives, who found an excellent way of life thanks to the workers who had to consider them as a lesser evil but convenient.

9

The politics in the XX Century

The twentieth century could have been a century of wars, conquests and agreements between countries as many others before, but there was a specific element that established the difference: Technology!

The Twentieth Century was an explosion of development over the foundations implanted in the previous century. We can see in the XIX Century the fall of the existent empires of Spain, Napoleonic France, Mughal in India and the Holy Roman Empire (the old *Sacrum Imperium Romanum*) to be substituted by the new empires of Russia, Britain, Germany, United States and Japan.

It was in the XIX Century when it seems that the door to the inventions was opened thanks to incredible minds as Thomas Alva Edison, Nikola Tesla, Alexander Graham Bell, James Watt, Samuel Morse and others. There was a shower of inventions: Telegraph and Morse code for communications, the electric motor, steam engine, telephone, photography, the light bulb and much more, as well as improvements and new applications.

The advances that reached to all sectors, including medicine, were astonishing in comparison with the discoveries of precedent centuries and were the seed for the even more incredible XX Century, where men got in touch with the atomic world, jumped to the space, went to the moon, sent space artifacts to other planets and covered our own space of satellites for several purposes.

All these changes and advances had to necessarily affect politics in the world as we will see.

We can divide the XX Century in two halves, the first one from the beginning until mid century and the second one, from mid century until the end and arrival of the year 2000.

Politics, in the first half was exuberant with a great abundance of leaders of all kind, for good and for bad as the new political systems.

Without a doubt, the most relevant by its transcendence was Communism, but let us first refer to the old and decadent Monarchy.

* * *

10

The Monarchy in the XX Century

We had already seen the abolitions of Monarchies occurred during the nineteenth Century in Mexico, France, the Mughal Empire in India, Parma, Modena, Tuscany and the Two Sicilies, Spain (only one year until restoration), Tahiti, Burma, Brazil, Thibaw Min, Hawaii and Madagascar.

During the 20th Century Monarchy continues declining with the disappearance of those of: Austria, Turkey, Spain again, Yugoslavia, Italy, Bulgaria, Albania, Romania, Egypt, China Empire, Vietnam, Tunisia, Iraq, North Yemen, Burundi, Libya, Cambodia, Greece, Ethiopia, Afghanistan, Laos and Iran.

Nevertheless the Monarchy as an institution continues existing nowadays, although and especially in the more developed countries, the person of the king or queen has lost relevance to become a representative figure with virtually no political responsibility, which is in the hands of the elected government.

The Monarchy as a form of government, although with the above mentioned limitations continues existing in Japan (as an empire) Great Britain, Netherlands, Sweden, Belgium, Denmark, Luxemburg (a Grand Duchy) Norway, Liechtenstein (principality), Monaco (principality), Morocco, Spain (returned again), Kuwait (as an emirate), Saudi Arabia, Malaysia, Thailand, UAE (formed by Emirates), Oman (a sultanate), Qatar (Emirate), Jordan, Bahrain (Emirate), Brunei (sultanate), Nepal, Cambodia, Swaziland, Bhutan, Lesotho, Tonga, Western Samoa (chiefdom).

The down fall of the Monarchy as it was known in the past is something unavoidable in our time, except in those countries, like Great Britain, where the presence of a king has something of romantic pride that does not interfere in the policy of the country.

11

Communism

Communism had its origin in the socio-economic theories expounded by Karl Marx in his work "The Capital" ("Das Kapital"). Karl Marx was a German philosopher born in Trier, Prusia on August 5th, 1818 and son of the lawyer Heinrich Marx of Jewish religion, who in 1824 converted with all his family to Catholicism.

Karl Marx obtained his doctorate in philosophy in Berlin in 1841; three years later he began a friendship with Friedrich Engels that lasted until his death in 1883.

His most famous work by its transcendence was "The Capital" that was published in three parts, the first of them was published in Hamburg in 1867; the second and the third one were published by Engels, when Marx had already died, in 1885 and 1894, respectively.

Marx considered that the feudal society had been substituted by the bourgeoisie that has softened the class antagonism, but at the same time he affirmed that the society was being divided more and more into two hostile sectors that oppose each other: the bourgeoisie and the proletariat.

Do you have clear the meaning and etymology of the word "proletariat"? Nick asked the class.

The proletariats are the workers, Abu said.

Nick waited some instants and as there was no reaction in the class, he continued.

Proletariat comes from "proletarius" a Latin word that in the old Roman civilization referred to the poorest class of people that couldn't give money to the State but only his children, that is to say, the "proles".

Continuing with Marx, he considered that the relations in society are dependent of the economy of market and this, on the existence of products and the market exchange, whose evolution of change depends on the products that each one has; this, in a primitive economy, will produce necessarily differences in the economic power of people; in an economy with currency, cash will oppose to merchandise in a permanent confrontation.

Marx in the chapter IV of "The Capital" presents the way how market circulates C-M-C (where C is cash (money) and M is any merchandise), that is to say cash buy merchandise and after the merchandise is sold and the cash recovered; and M-C-M where somebody sells merchandise getting cash and afterwards use the cash to buy merchandise again.

That presentation of the market looks elemental; I would say that is almost child-like because it looks only the surface of the operations without getting more into everyday life situations.

Money (cash) buy merchandise and after the merchandise is sold by money, but that does not restore things to its original situation, because besides the possible surplus, money can go to different hands or even can produce a loss or a lower value.

Marx understood that the operation C-M-C has not sense because what is pursued is the other C-M-$\underline{C}'$ where $C' = C+X$, being X a surplus or benefit. It is this variable value X what will form contingents of capital.

If we continue considering the movement of money to buy merchandise, we will find two alternatives of which only one will be to generate capital and is when the products obtained by money are not needed and will be used to change again to money, but to a higher amount than when the merchandise was bought.

The other possibility is to use money to buy consumer products needed for life as food, clothing or others, in such a case, the products will not be sold again but consumed and they will not generate capital, on the contrary, it will reduce the capital of the consumer although it will increase the capital of those who sold the merchandise.

Well, this conception of the market presenting two opposed kind of people together with the demagogic speech of politicians and union leaders, was a poison to society. Now when workers are better off than ever, they hate their employers more than ever before.

In 1848 being in Brussels, Marx prepared together with Engels the Communist Manifesto that was published in German the same year under the name of "Manifest der Kommunistischen Partei"; this had repercussion in all Europe. Since them the confrontation between workers and employers, left and right, liberals and conservatives is as irreconcilable as their own naiveté, letting them to be dragged by the deceptive rhetoric of politicians that foster for their own convenience this antagonism between classes.

What does the money can buy? Merchandise, farm or handicraft products, but the farm products were cultivated and harvested by workers and the handicraft products were manufactured by the artisan and his workers.

This take us to consider that before the mentioned operation C-M-C or in its contrary form M-C-M have to be a previous of C-W (Money-Worker) namely the investment in workers that will continue until the moment of the harvest when it will produce the completion of the operation when the cash investment get a return in products that will be put in the market and will be changed by money. What I just said is valid for both products; those from the field and those from a factory where in order to be in capacity to offer them for sale it is necessary first to invest in workers and raw materials.

Do you think that the capital is a decisive factor in market operations? Nick asked.

Well, in my opinion as important as capital or money are the products of any kind that can be purchased with money, because money is a tool of exchange if there is not available merchandise that could be changed for money, this has no value. Rag pointed.

That is a point to consider, Nick accepted, but in your opinion having to choose between money and merchandise, which is more important?

In my opinion, Rag continued, merchandise is more important. Let us suppose that you are lost in a desert or in any other arid area, you are alone without hope to be found or finding somebody and you have with you a handbag full of money. Does the money be of any help to you? Now let's suppose that instead of money the bag contains food and water. What situation would you prefer?

It is a good reasoning Nick said.

These economic concepts of Marx about the market process focuses too much on the unfavorable position of the workers in front to the power of the capital that was supposed to be the motor of the market process, ran like gunpowder throughout Europe among labor groups wakening the always latent resentments from workers to business-owners, that has more of envy, lack of knowledge and wrong focusing of the problem than of reality.

Workers do not think about the background of the problem, they only see the surface of it that for them is: "they have it and I don't have it". Can we imagine a more simplistic way of thinking?

The fact that some people have and others do not is a reality, but why? What is the reason for this situation? Every effect has always a cause. If ideally we take a group of people without money, of the same social family condition and we give to each one of them the same amount of money so that they evolve and reproduce that money for their life, sure, absolutely sure that if after some time we analyze the outcome of the experiment we could understand why there are rich and poor people. I think this is easy for anybody to understand.

Returning to Marx, of course it was not easy to break the inertia of centuries of same governments, but with his theories the fuses had been lit and continued running, it was only necessary a person to materialize the theory into a real movement and this was Vladimir Ilyich Ulyanov, best known as Lenin (1870-1924), resentful after the execution of his brother, he became a political theorist that supported the concepts expressed by Marx and Engels and their Communist Manifesto of 1848.

Also the soil was fertile during the First World War to receive such ideas, especially in Russia where the war had produced a terrible economic situation to which were added the wrong decisions of the Tsar that created great inflation to the point that people were hungry, mainly in big cities.

In 1917 (in March of our calendar) the first revolution was produced in the capital, then Petrograd (Saint Petersburg). The Tsar Nicholas II was removed and the Provisional Government was installed, headed by Alexander Kerensky.

Constant mass protests, strikes and mutinies of every faction made the Provisional Government unstable and turbulent, because it was constantly disturbed by the different factions of the lowers classes represented by the soviets and also soon by the middle class of the cities to the point that in fact we can say that the power was divided and the faction that was getting increasingly more power were the Bolsheviks led by Lenin, who had the ability to employ the always magic words to motivate people: land for the peasants and food for the workers, without forgetting a problem of national concern: to end the participation of Russia in the First World War, this promise in opposition to the

Provisional Government which had decided to continue the war.

Each time more consolidated, the Bolsheviks organized their followers integrated mainly by workers in a militia under their control that they named the Red Guards.

In October (November of Gregorian calendar) a Second Revolution of the Bolsheviks happened led by Lenin to overthrow the Provisional Government, establishing the government of the *Sovnarkom*. In March 1918 the Treaty of Brest-Litovsk was signed with Germany ending Russia's participation in the IWW and in that same year the capital of the country was moved to Moscow. To ensure the security of the government the Bolscheviks created the *Checa* a sort of intelligence service, an organism to punish anyone that could be considered an enemy of the people.

The several factions existing at the moment in Russia were confronted in a civil war, with the participation of the Bolsheviks "Reds" and the Tsarists Russians "Whites" who defending the old system, attempted to crush the movement acting as counter-revolutionaries, other not well defined movements promoted independence, and finally the socialist non-Bolsheviks.

The Bolsheviks won, and in 1922 the Union of Soviet Socialist Republics (USSR) was created, the Tsar and his family were executed and a new era began in Russia. The government was in the hands of one party, which was much more authoritarian than any of the old regimes. The new government renamed the country as The Soviet Union and was headed by Lenin until 1924 when he died.

During almost one hundred years Russians suffered the most authoritarian dictatorship that ever existed on earth, from the beginning of the known time. The outcome is that when the Soviet Union collapsed, the mass of people was hungry and oppressed, while those connected to the government left the country buying mansions and opening big business in several western countries.

Did people learn from this experience? No, people continue believing in the unbelievable and suffering for their naivety because no matter how bad the past experience could be, there are thousands of people that continue believing in communism.

*　*　*

12

Fascism

The fascism groups, a series of ideologies that flourished in the first half of the XX Century, which in some country as it was the case of Spain lasted until the last quarter of the century.

Who can remember the origin of the name? Nick asked to the class.

Lora Lord raised her hand and began: The name comes from the "fasces" ported by the lictors in the old Roman civilization, tradition received from the Etruscan civilization. The lictors carried the fasces before the magistrate in the legions parades. The fasces were a group of wood staves tied in the middle, from which it used to be emerging an axe.

Very well Lora, Nick said, you are well aware.

Then Nick continued. Fascism began in Italy with the National Fascist Party of Benito Mussolini, who at a certain moment had the dream of bringing back Italy to the glory of the ancient Roman Empire. Precisely the term "fascist" comes from "fasces" that, as Lora explained, were a bundle of rods, which in Italy meant a group of labor union associations.

From the beginning, Adolf Hitler was an admirer of Mussolini to whom alluded in his book "Mein Kampf". In their moment, Fascist movements in the rest of Europe were a reaction against Communism to avoid its proliferation, as well as those pseudo communist Socialist movements, which otherwise would have invaded Europe. Fascism, apart from Italy, appeared in Germany, Austria, Greece, Poland, Romania, Croatia, Portugal, Spain, Hungary and Norway with longer or shorter duration, which was also affected by the evolution of the 2nd WW. In Portugal and Spain, which remained neutral in the Second WW it had a longer life.

In the countries where its transcendence was more relevant, we can find some peculiarities as was the racism in Germany, as well as an attempt to expand it beyond its borders, this last characteristic was also found in Italy. In the remainder countries the relevant feature was an exacerbation of nationalism.

In Germany in spite of its obvious similarities, it was not used the term "Fascism" but "Nazism".

As always, religion had a role in these movements. While the Spanish "Falange" and the "Estado Novo" of Portugal were extremely Christian, in other countries there was not such a high fervor and in Germany it could be seen attempts to devote old historic and forgotten cults.

Who has an opinion about why this political system appeared in the political arena?

You said that was a reaction against communist proliferation. Abu said.

Yes, Nick answered, but it is good to find all the roots, I would dare to say that fascism in Europe was a continuation of the former authoritarian monarchies. People during centuries were used to obey under the unquestionable oppression of the church, the king was not God like in ancient times, but his realm supposed to have the favor of God, otherwise he wouldn't be there.

The French Revolution and the industrial revolution were a very strong influence in the minds of people tired of tradition, which means feudalism, religion, kingship and a-buse and more abuse, they wanted a change but did not lose the habit of obeying; and fascism taking from the old Roman Empire the proud of nationalism added a new element to people: patriotism, there was an exaltation of the national values, in each country according their idiosyncrasy.

I would like to know your opinion about the significance of Fascism in the 20th Century, as well as your comments of its transcenddence, if any, in today's political world.

Nick looked around and saw three arms raised, he pointed to Emily.

In my opinion, he said, Fascism, in any of its forms, was a sample of authoritarian government that is not acceptable in our time.

What do you mean? Interrupted Gregory, Are you saying that the people of a country do not have the right of choosing the kind of government they desire?

No, if it is to oppress its citizens. Emily answered.

That is only something you are supposing. What happens if in a general and free elections people choose that system? Gregory continued.

That they are wrong! Emily ended.

Everybody has the right of making a mistake, even you can be wrong in something and not because of that other people has the right of interfering in your life. Gregory pointed out.

I see another aspect of the analysis, Lora Lord said, apart from the quality of the system, I think that all happens how and when must happen. None of you took into consideration that if all those nationalist movements did not appear, possibly the world would be now living under a terrible communist dictatorship?

In my humble opinion those movements of fascist character, the 2nd WW and the intervention of the United States of America saved the world, unless some of you are able to demonstrate that a general communist dictatorship would have been better for people, demonstration that in my opinion is not possible.

You can see, continued Lora, how during all the post war period, and even today, there are all over the world, people and even some countries that believe in communism, no matter the evidence of its failure, of its abuse on people, of its absence of human rights, of the corruption of its governors, people continue seeing white what evidently is black.

That is a good consideration Lora, Nick said. It has sense!

But professor, I want to clarify that in spite of what I said, that does not mean that I approve the expansionist policy of Italy or Germany or the crimes committed by this last one.

I understand that, Nick said, any other comment?

You asked also about the possible transcendence of the existence of fascism, if any, in today's political world, said Rag, there is no doubt that any event of any kind that happens in the world left a imprint and it will be remembered.

Being conscious of the variegated human nature, the memory of those events will produce a different effect in the minds of people. For some of them it will be a bad nightmare that has to be forgotten, but some others, they only will see favorable aspects that they would want to reinstate and they attempt to do it even against a majority that could be thinking otherwise.

That is, in my opinion, the transcendence of the existence of Fascism in our today's life. A bad influence!

Well, Nick said, we have made a brief exam of this political system enough to have a comprehension of its political meaning in the comparison that unavoidably we will do with the other systems for our political analysis.

We are a little late but I think we can still talk about Democracy

13

Democracy

We are now going to talk of the best seller of the political systems, in modern and contemporary political theory there is not a better system for people in general than democracy, because under a capitalist atmosphere it gives possibility to any citizen to get a high level position and comfort in society.

Contrarily to communism that does not give citizens any opportunity of progressing, democracy has specific rules that work as a social contract between citizens and State. In democratic states supposedly governed by law, it is common the existence of what is named a Constitution, that acts as a Bill of Rights to citizens and a warranty to the functioning of the State, highlighting the basic principles that will make possible the communal living and subordinated to its rules is the law that affects and obliges all citizens without distinction of any kind.

Nick saw Gregory making a gesture of doubt and said: I know Gregory that in its application there are distinctions, but we will talk about that when we comment the failures of the system. Now we have to continue.

In democracy there are three powers that to be effective must be autonomous and act separately: First, the executive branch that takes the necessary internal and external political decisions and is the government properly said. Second, the legislative branch that produces the legal system and discuses political problems issuing the necessary laws to maintain the proper functioning of the State; and third, the judicial branch that knows about the violations of the law and according with the law, applies the punishment for each violation.

We can say that the legislative and judicial powers are complementary to the executive, because at the time that complete the activity of the State can be an element of control of the executive in systems that are in good working order.

The parts in this social contract have not only rights but also duties, let us see:

The government has to provide the necessary means to the education of the population in all its levels in order to get good professionals that will contribute to the development of the country.

It will provide also medical assistance, accessible to all citizens and foreign residents, as well as social security for those who after having worked during all their life have to retire and need to receive all kind of assistance. Safe living in any community of the country provided by all the institutions that care for the internal and external security and will take in consideration any other necessary measures to keep people calm and convinced that they are living well and consequently that is good to support the functioning of the State in what could be possible for each citizen.

The facilities the State must provide reach even to those that are not a living necessity as is entertainment. This is very important and was taken into account through the whole history of the world: Olympic Games, circus, gladiators, theatre, dance, movies, all the variety of sports and nowadays we have to add also some electronic games.

Why do you think that could be important to care for the entertainment of people? Nick asked to the class.

Barbara raised her hand and said: So that they have a break from their daily work.

I think that it is something of more interest to the State, George Lin said, in my opinion it is possible that promoting entertainment for people, the State is thinking to make them happy, but with the hidden purpose of protecting its own stability, because while people have their thoughts occupied by sports or other exhibitions is less critic with politics.

You were almost in target, but now the great question, Nick said looking at the students. Do you think that with all the advantages we mentioned people live happy now under democracy?

No, answered several voices.

No? Nick asked, why no?

Rag answered, because the traditional and natural unconformity of people that always desire more or a different thing, no matter how well they could be, this frequently takes them to mistakes of terrible consequences for the country and of course for them.

It is not only that, Lora said, I do not agree in blaming only to the people because many of them suffer deficiencies of the system.

What deficiencies? Nick asked.

Many deficiencies, I don't mind if they are more or less than in other systems, people suffer for that.

You have to justify your asseveration, Nick insisted, otherwise it has no value. Mention some of those deficiencies you find to analyze them and arrive to a conclusion.

Deficiencies of Democracy
Political Parties

Well, Lora said, everybody knows that the political parties are by themselves a deficiency in the democratic system, in spite of what they could announce; their main interest is not people or the country itself but power, that is to say, to win and control the State.

Before these democratic times the political parties had, at least in theory, an ideology destined to the welfare of the country, no matter if due to any circumstance they do not succeed in their purpose or the ruler was pursuing other kind of interest, the majority of the members believed in that ideology. Today, if you stop in the street to a member of a political party and ask him about the ideology of his party you can be sure that in most of the cases, he does not know what to answer and in many others it doesn't exist.

But that it is not the only deficiency of democracy, it is certain that if something is good in theory not necessarily will be good in practice, so to give to every citizen the right of voting to designate a new ruler for the State, seems a fair decision although goes against what logic says.

If we were asked about who could make the best decision about anything, there is no doubt that we would say the best prepared and the most intelligent, and that is true.

How is elected the most important and transcendental position in a democratic country? The election of a new president who will rule the destiny of each and all of citizens is made with the general vote of all citizens, which looks fair, nevertheless it is known that in all countries, I would say without exception, the highest percentage of population is integrated for those less educated, prepared and knowledgeable in spite of the mandatory dispositions of governments enforcing the duty of education since the childhood. Even more, in any country of what is named third world, the unprepared people reach more than half of the population, not only by their lack of preparation but also by their bad fortune, what make them easy prey for unscrupulous people that get their votes with good speeches, money or promises.

What is the result? Countries subjugated by all kind of crooks who makes people suffer and burglarize the country until its total destruction. I do not need to give examples, everyone here knows several.

And these are not the only deficiencies, I can find several others.

All right Lora, Nick said, we will analyze now these two failures and then you can continue.

One first shortcoming of democracy according with Lora is political parties. Who has any opinion on the matter? Asked Nick to the class.

Rag raised his hand and said: I'm afraid I have to agree with Lora in what refers to political parties. What produces the good functioning of a country is not the person of its president by itself but all the system in its three branches, integrated for thousands of individuals, if they accomplish their function.

If we agree on the importance of the experience in people, the stability of public servants, it is important if they are working well, they will already have a good knowledge of his duty what will contribute to the good and efficient development of the country, but when a new political party wins, many of the public workers, if they are not protected by the administrative system, are changed or at least their directors will be changed, what it is not good for the country.

Excuse me Rag, Albert interrupted, don't you think that to keep directors of a former political party would be like to have enemies inside the house that can do their best to reduce, as far as possible, the efficiency of the opposing party?

I understand the matter is complex, because both alternatives have a risk, Rag said, the same as with directors could happen with the rest of public workers, who if they are from an opposition party, can be a disturbing element. Possibly this gives the reason to Lora in his theory that political parties are a weakness in the system. I have not an answer now and I need to think about, may be we can discus it later, Rag said.

Other inconvenience of a system based on political parties, Rag continued, is that favors the increase in bureaucracy, each time more and more administrative departments are created, each party is by itself a source of bureaucracy; besides that, the political party which has won the election, has to find positions for its followers.

This increase of administration offices affects negatively the economy of the country although it favors deceitfully, the statistics of employment for the new party in power. We must not forget the lack of productivity of many of those workers who feel themselves protected by the party and with the right to be employed.

It's all right, Nick said. Somebody else who can comment on the other failure exposed by Lora, related to the election system generally adopted.

George Lin raised his hand again and began to say: It is difficult to talk against something that looks the fairest thing in politics, namely, the right of each one to express his opinion as a citizen, but unfortunately, Lora is right, this is a good sample about the difference between theory and practice and the election system as is now applied in the majority of the countries produces unwanted results.

In my opinion something has to be done to avoid that people could be deceived because of the enormous transcendence of such deception. In the last sixty years we can find an important number of countries that have suffered the consequences of that evil.

Would you propose something? Nick asked.

I would need to think about, because it is not easy. I think that even pretending to be fair and respecting the freedom of people, the first North American rulers understood the problem and to control it in part, organized their system of electoral colleges in each State, which I don't know if it is effective enough, but the important thing for us in this class is that the problem effectively exists and has to be taken into account.

Now Lora, you can continue with the other deficiencies you wanted to expose.

Thank you, Lora said, I will also include other deficiency of political parties that nowadays configure one of the most terrible events we can find worldwide in the political activity: Corruption.

Political corruption

Corruption affects now, in higher or lower degree, to almost all countries and not only affects the prestige of the political party of the crook, but the country in general and to its citizens in particular, economically, socially and morally due to the bad example that represents.

What is the problem with corruption? For more than half a century it has been proliferating and continues in crescendo. Why? Because in spite of what could be said, there is not an interest to eliminate it.

Corruption is like a poisonous fluid that has invaded the whole world. I think that could be written a full book about that.

You are right, Nick said, political corruption does harm greatly the credibility of any political system, doing that people, each one in his level, cease to believe in the system or try to do the same seeing how the majority of the corrupts go unpunished.

In some countries under the pressure of the public opinion and to avoid disrepute to the party, great affaires are being discovered and the corrupt subdued to public judgment. Rag ended.

But, which are, in your opinion, the causes of corruption? Nick asked to the class, Go give me a reason.

Lack of honesty in people, Roger said, but corruption does not affect only to democracy but to any other system, even though I don't know if in democracy is more abundant or it goes more unpunished.

Frederic: Vanishing of the sense of honor, people don't care if they are called thieves.

Barbara: Lack of punishment, most of corrupts walk among us instead of being in prison, and the lack of punishment is because current rulers do not punish corrupts because it could be a precedent that could be applied later to them.

Abu: Perhaps corruption is a natural instinct in humans.

Sarah: I agree with Barbara it is the lack of a proportional punishment; criminals do not fear the law.

Rag: I think an important cause of corruption is the enormous offer of consumer goods that people want to have no matter how, even though the problem is always in people and the offer is only a motivation to stimulate their bad instincts.

Arnold: It's the social competition; people want to have a better thing than his neighbor or friend has.

It is enough, Nick said, all what you have said is true. Effectively there is a large offer of any kind of products that goes from useful things at home until unnecessary luxury products that are wanted for the mass of population and people would do anything, legal or not, to get them, which means a lack of honesty, but for many people the way how they get the products or the money to buy them is not important because, as you said, they have lost the sense of honesty.

Why some people act in that way when they have the opportunity? Because it is the reaction produced by the personal struggle between their natural instincts and the obligation to respect the law for a great part of humans who want to be free without any conditioning, even more knowing how many of them are unpunished enjoying the result of their lack of honesty.

Lora, do you want to comment something more? Nick asked.

Well, Lora said, besides corruption or as another aspect of it, there is another deficiency coming from people outside the party that in some way give large amounts of money to help the party in its promotion and advertising, money that really constitute an investment if the political party wins, in which case the money will be largely recovered in several kind of favors, among which expensive public works are an important part.

Other important aspect that has no sense for me is that in the majority of the countries; the government gives to each political party a substantial amount of money each year to contribute to cover its expenses, why?

The foundation of a political party requires that the founder must present a specific quantity of signatures of citizens that support the legalization of the party, what is easy to get because there are always people willing to support any new idea when there is someone with an easy and promising speech promoting the new organization.

Some of the supporters do that convinced they are doing something good, others find that it is an opportunity to grow, to dedicate their activity to the party from the beginning. Are any of those people thinking in the country? No, they are thinking in themselves and little by little the party becomes a great administrative apparatus integrated by people who live of it waiting the moment when, through a general election, they have the opportunity of ruling the country and to obtain more important positions. Of course all that people will do their best to defend the continuation of the party because it rep-resents their own subsistence.

Until the moment when a party achieve to win, its main activity is to open centers of representation in all the country and to promise and promise, no matter what, any-thing that makes people to dream in a new life for them, with more wealth and more opportunities because they are never satis-fied.

Of course that permanent contribution of the government to political parties has the support of every one of them and of its members because they live from the party. It goes without saying that this great contribution is, as usual, paid by all citizens in their taxes.

It is normal that any citizen conscious of a bad administration in the country and considering him capable of ruling the country and to contribute to its development, do his/her best to try to win in the next elections.

It is also normal, that hearing his speech a more or less important number of people supports and follows the proposals for a new government. Then, the candidate can succeed or not, which will depend of several factors.

What is not normal is that somebody thinks in creating a new party and all citizens have to pay for it, even the opponents.

That has a reason of being, interrupted Gregory, as far as I know, the main reason of the sponsorship of the government to political parties is to avoid that they are sponsored by third parties that afterwards, will attempt to recover their money in advantages of many kinds.

That's stupid, Lora said, everybody knows that all over the world, in one or other way, political parties receive money of great manufactures, oil companies, builders, banks or financial organizations that parties cannot forget if they win the election.

You are suggesting that sometimes the speech of those political promoters is deceiving and false, how people can do to protect themselves of the effect of that discourse? Gregory asked.

It is not so easy, Lora answered, because the suggestion that the warming of the speech or a sensible discourse produces in people, as well as the promises of things really needed by the population or the promise of changing situations that are adversely affecting a majority of people, promises that at first people believe that it will be accomplished.

In summary, in my opinion, Lora continued, political parties are a dead weight to the country, divide the population in sectors against each other, each member does not think in the welfare of the country but of him and besides political parties increase bureaucracy, a corrosive element in any country.

You have made a large exposition and have shown your opinion on the matter, Nick said.

Is there anybody else who wanted to add something about political parties?

There was not answer and Nick continued.

Do you have any further comment about Democracy?

I think that Democracy, Lora said, if the above mentioned deficiencies can be fixed, would be the best political system to this date.

Do you really think that those deficiencies can be corrected or suppressed? Nick asked.

No, I don't think so; because people at this time show that they are unable to understand that they could be free and at the same time submitted to something although this could be the law.

Then, Nick asked again, has this situation remedy or not?

Everything can have a remedy; the difficulty is to achieve it. In this case we are not talking of a make up or of a simple change but of a deep change that will affect to all levels of people and it will produce international political alterations, nevertheless it has already timidly began with the international alliances.

Gregory raised his hand and said: professor, I made an observation at the beginning with respect to your comment that the law affects and obliges all citizens without distinction of any kind...

That's all right, go ahead.

I think that the equality of people in front of the law is only a charming theory and only that; everybody knows that except some specific cases that cannot be hidden, the usual is that the actions of people of prestige have a different treatment that if they come from any unknown person.

In the old Greece cradle of democracy it seems that things worked well under that system. I have two questions that I ask myself: first, if the system was as good as is said, why did not proliferate and needed around two millennia to be reinstated again in the world? And second, why has now all that deficiencies that were commented here?

The reasons are simple, Nick said, to your first question about why democracy had to wait two millennia to proliferate; I would say that the old Greek democracy did not return or it will return.

The students looked at him with curiosity.

Yes that's true, the old democracy died in the old Greece and never returned. Its first obstacle was the growth of the cities, the over population, that avoided the possibility of a personal direct voting about any proposition.

Our new democracy has of the old democracy only the name that politicians knew that was very suggestive to people, don't you think so? "The government of people" for that reason the present democracy is named "representative" that is to say, people govern but represented by the politicians, a sector of people that have arrogated to them, without any justification, the art of govern. It is true that those persons that represent the people are voted by them but the reality is that many people not even know their names.

The clue of success is to permit people as much as possible, freedom, total freedom from children to elders, which was a transitory solution for transitory governors but at the same time it is a time bomb for a near future, because as people never are or will be satisfied, having a so great capacity of free action they want more, and following the advising of miserable demagogues will bring the destruction to the State.

About the reason of the deficiencies we have found, are the results of the circumstances of our present way of living.

George Lin raised his hand and said: Do you have any suggestion that contribute to remedy this situation?

Yes, which does not mean that could be easy to implant, just the submission to the law under fair laws, fair judges and without any distinction about who is who, everybody, no matter if it is the president of the country or the sweeper of the street, because both must have same value in front of the law.

Corrections are not difficult when they really want to be done, so what is necessary is the will of doing it.

Really it is not so easy, George commented.

No, because in fact is the construction of a new world. Nick finished.

14

Great alliances:
The European Union

Nick arrived to the class and all murmur of students talking among them faded out. Nick began.

Since the middle of the 20th Century a new order of things appeared like a new phenomenon in politics, after the exaltation of nationalisms in the first half of the Century, it began to appear a tendency to coexistence among countries and in Europe took place the idea of something that at the beginning was only referred to commerce and little by little it became a community of countries with the same currency and without borders, but before we continue with this explanation, I would like to know your opinion about what was the reason of that change of things, from a close nationalism to a policy of opening, with a tendency to a possible globalization.

Arnold Man asked to speak said: For me it is very clear, the reason of that change was the desire for peace after the terrible experience of the Second World War. That desire was manifested especially in Europe and Japan where the suffering had been more intense.

Gregory raised his hand and said: I agree in part with Arnold, but in my opinion other factors also influenced that change and the principal one was a tendency to freedom perhaps originated in events apparently unimportant, but with a great transcendence as it was the Hippie movement that made a reality the behavior of those Bohemians we could find in Paris in the 19th century.

Hippies began to revive that liberal way of thinking, this time with more success, at the beginning of the second half of the 20th century in the United States or Great Britain, and spread it around the world with the banner of freedom and ignoring all social conventionalisms, using drugs, playing music and manufacturing small ornamental crafts, to survive in a communal living in which they share all.

Good, Nick began, you have expressed two different opinions both possibly valid. The opinion of Arnold is true because after the Second World War, which did not last long, but with terrible effects, people were anxious for peace, they wanted to forget and have fun. One of the successful songs after the war was "La vie en rose" and with regard to the desires

138

for freedom commented by Gregory, it is very possible that such desires consolidated in vast sectors a tendency to live each one according to his will, not tied up to rules or compromises and this could have been a spark that favored the good relationship among countries and the beginning of large alliances.

The desire for peace gave its fruit: around seventy years of reasonable peace in the world, except for the permanent confrontation between Israelis and Palestinians, something unavoidable for anybody who reasons well and several other local confrontations. Who can mention some of such confrontations?

George Lin raised his hand and began to say: In my opinion, the reason for which we have had 70 years of peace, very relative by the way, it was because during the Cold War EEUU and URSS were linked by the MAD (mutually assured destruction). Nevertheless there were many conflagrations beginning by Korea, then Vietnam, several others in African and South American countries in the majority of the cases with EEUU or URSS backing opposing sides, without forgetting the eight years of war between Irak and Iran and the two wars between EEUU and Irak, The terrible civil war in Siria and ISIS as an insurgent terrorist group that has terrified the world specially in Europe and its assassinations in Midle East and Africa.

Very good George, although when we were talking of peace we were referring to the interval elapsed without a new world war.

Then looking at the class said: What is in your opinion the cause of that large period without a generalized conflagration, do you think that was the memory of the last WW?

I think that is not enough, it must be something more. Sarah said.

Yes there is something more, Nick approved, but what is it?

Nick saw three hands up: Rag, Roger and Lora, he pointed to Rag.

I do not believe the states were at peace because the memory of the war, along the history of the world, war and fights were constant when some country found itself stronger than the opponent, there is something else and I think that was fear, yes, the fear to the new powerful weapons that had been tested recently in Hiroshima and Nagasaki, which after the war, in a short period of time were in the hands of several countries.

Good, Nick said, I think that is the reason. Now let us continue.

The idea of a multilateral association of countries began to be worked out in Europe and also it had started in South America in the times of Simon Bolivar, but there the project did not crystallize and in Europe it was a matter of many years of meetings and discussions that deserve more detailed information.

The first proposals and approaches in Europe for community integration can be found in 1946 at the end of the Second World War with the suggestion of Winston Churchill about the creation of a United States of Europe, which was followed in 1949 by the organization of the European Counsel.

The following step that began, although little by little to crystallize the project was the ECSC (European Coal and Steel Community) proposed in 1950 by the French Foreign Minister Robert Schuman, possibly with the purpose to avoid a new contest between France and Germany, affirming that this would make war between them impossible.

The ECSC was established in the Treaty of Paris of 1951 signed for France, West Germany, Belgium, Italy, Netherlands and

Luxembourg, came into force in 1952 and was a common market of coal and steel among the members and a little relief for Germany to whom some of the vetoes imposed after the war were lifted, it was also the first International Organization with supranational regulations.

For the operation and administration of the treaty, the corresponding agencies as the *High Authority* that could correspond to the actual *European Commission* and the Assembly now the *European Parliament* were established.

The same "Six" in the Treaty of Rome celebrated in 1957 founded the EEC (<u>European Economic Community</u>) and a customs union. In the same treaty they created the European Atomic Energy Community (Euratom) establishing rules of cooperation for the development of Nuclear Energy. Both treaties came into force in 1958.

This new platform for a European unification, among others, had to face two stalemates with France, the first one in 1954 by France refusing to ratify the European defense project that had been signed two years before, because the France of de Gaulle wanted to maintain its army organization independent. The second one was in 1960 when the United

Kingdom together with other six countries created the *Free Commerce European Association* in opposition to the *European Economic Community,* and France perhaps afraid of the power that seemed to be acquiring de EEC attempted to reduce the supranational power of the community, which originated tensions among the members.

On its side the United Kingdom conscious of the progress of the EEC applied to become a member in 1961, but Charles de Gaulle was opposed to its entry, and the United Kingdom couldn't be accepted until de Gaulle was out of the French government.

France and West Germany Tried without success of establishing a headquarters for the EEC in what it was named *The Sarre Statute* that it was rejected in the referendum celebrated in the place.

The tensions originated from 1960 specially with France by its insistence in reducing the supranational power and by its refusal to accept the United Kingdom in the community, it was apparently solved from 1965 onwards, when it was decided to merge the three communities, which was done with the *Merger Treaty* celebrated in Brussels and in force from the first of July of 1967, where it was created a unique agency for the three communities that was named *European Communities*, which adopted a common custom tariff in all the community for imports from other countries

In 1973, the adhesion to the Treaty of Denmark and Greenland, Ireland and the United Kingdom was produced. Greenland due to problems related to the fishing rights left the community in 1985.

In 1979, the European Monetary System that later on will arrive to the adoption of a single currency was established.

In 1981 Greece signed the treaty.

In 1985 the Schengen Agreement established the basis for removing passport controls in borders among member States, and some others.

In 1986 Portugal and Spain joined the treaty and the use of the European Flag in the community was adopted.

In 1990 after the fall of the Berlin Wall, East Germany was added to the Union, enlarging the community territory although not the number of countries.

The first of November of 1993 came into force the *Maastricht Treaty* where the European Union was created.

In 1995 Austria, Finland and Sweden were accepted in the European Union.

In 1999 the European Union suffered a crisis refusing the Parliament to approve the management of the 1996 *Santer Commission,* which resigned the same day. For that reason an agency of control against the fraud (OLAF) to avoid such happenings was created.

In the 2002 the monetary systems of the twelve States members were substituted by the Euro.

In 2004 ten new members joined the EU: Cyprus, Czech Republic, Estonia, Hungary, Latvia, Lithuania, Malta, Poland, Slovakia and Slovenia.

In 2007 two new members joined the EU: Bulgaria and Romania.

In 2009 came into force the Treaty of Lisbon that introduced several modifications to the structure of the Union.

In 2013 The European Union accepted its 28th member: Croatia.

The European Union had to face several problems due to the monetary crisis in some southern countries, but the worse one was the result of a referendum in the United Kingdom of June 23 of 2016, where the citizens decided to leave the European Union, this was the famous "Brexit" that was notified to the European Union and now is in a process that will end in 2019.

This is a brief summary of the first important alliance in the world that in my opinion is the germ of the world's future, that is to say a Great World Confederation.

Now let me have your comments about this important integration event.

I think it is not easy to put in agreement so many people, we are talking of around 570 million people, Abu said, the proof is that it is beginning to crumble, the Brexit is just the beginning.

I do not agree with you, Barbara argued, in my opinion is a very important effort that until now has demonstrated that integration is possible, of course this is the first attempt and possibly many aspects need to be considered and modified.

George Lin requested to speak and said: The European Community is something very important never achieved before in the world, only for that deserves my respect. It is not necessary to say that it has several failures not easy to solve, because every country is jealous of its sovereignty, but that are essential for a definitive success.

Which are in your opinion those failures, Nick asked.

Well, continued George, the basic failure is the lack of a government with authority to enforce the rules and regulations established and approved, this capacity must include, if necessary, the use of coercive means.

In case a member decides for any reason to abandon the Community, independently of the procedure of separation that most are well established, from the moment they announce formally its separation, it must lose the prerogatives of member and have to be considered a non member with all that it entails, because if it is permitted to participate in some of the commercial advantages for the members, this would be a bad example, almost an invitation for others to do the same.

The quality of member must be something on which members and citizens have to be proud of and consider an honor to be accepted for all the advantages and safety that it represents.

I don't need to say that it is not acceptable the proliferation of crimes or the abuse of people in the territories of the community; and all members must be responsible of their territory, if they are unable to control crime, the Community will have the right of intervention and the capability to judge the guilty, independently of his/her nationality to eliminate a possible proliferation in other territories, because the quality of member of the community must prevail on the other of origin.

Until here it is the easy part, more complex is the activity of the community towards the exterior, that is to say, with the other non member countries. It must be organized to have a friendly relationship with the other countries, considering always that the first interest to defend is that of the community, but also prepared to face any aggression and being in capacity to win, which supposes the existence of a community army. An unarmed country is at the mercy of any other led by an unconscionable.

Another aspect that deserves consideration is the absence of borders, as far as I know some countries of the community have been facing problems by the movement of criminals and terrorists among the territories of the states members. It will be more rational to keep borders in each territory although the passage would be free to the members; these points of control would be attended by the Community Police and will permit a sort of control for those circulating by them that now it is not possible.

Also, in the several fields related to Science or to the mind, the community will have to establish central organisms of investigation in order to join and profit the efforts and a-chievements of all country members and to make the community each time stronger.

Congratulations George, Nick approved, you have improvised a good proposition of amend-ment.

George nodded thanking the comment of the professor.

Nick continued, now we are going to pay attention and analyze a problem that, along with terrorism, is one of the first challenges to face in this new XXI Century: Populism.

*　*　*

15

The Populism of the XXI Century

First of all, Nick said, giving a glance to the students, what is populism?

Several hands rose and Nick pointed to Gregory.

In my opinion it is a deceiving political activity based on flattering people to get their votes.

Do you think that is necessarily a deceiving policy?

Absolutely, because a fair policy does not need to flatter anybody, what they do is to say that all that exists in the country is bad and stimulate hate between the various sectors of population.

Now Nick pointed to Sarah who had also raised her hand.

I think populism is a sort of policy that consists in exalting the differences between social classes to obtain the support of the lower classes, presenting to them false solutions that never gets to become true. I said "a sort of policy" because to me it is not a doctrine or a political system but a political fraud.

Then Nick invited Rag to talk.

Knowing human nature, we cannot think that populism is something that appeared yesterday, it has always existed when the political conditions permit it. Now it has a very typical connotation, that is to say, to profit the naivety and discomfort of the lower social stamens, to use them in its favor to reach political power.

Regarding only the name, we find in the United States of America the "People's Party" (1892/1896) whose members were called "populists" and reached a 10% of the population until the Presidential elections of 1896 when they joined the Democratic Party and disappeared merged with it. Nevertheless its shade was not the same as that of the actual populist movements.

What is populism for you Lora? Nick asked.

Obviously, Lora said, populists do not like that connotation, we the other people, are who have to identify them as such, and we do that by the characteristic way they develop the promotion of their policy using in their favor the deficiencies that a sector of the population is suffering, as well as their way of governing relying on part of the population and promoting hate against the rest.

It is difficult for the people of a country avoid to fall in such trick because the populists will maintain their speech of promises until the end as they know that they have to fight in the democratic arena and have to win in a general elections, this is important because it ensures them legitimacy at least for some time until the moment the damage to the country and people can't be hidden, but even then they blame other State or their opponents and continue having support of their followers to whom they compensate with some small hand outs to keep their favor.

Now if I have to give a definition of Populism I would say that it consists in a pseudo-political speech addressed to the less favored classes of a country, encouraging them against the most favored elite with the promise that it will be destroyed and that will be destroyed by them, the poor people who will enjoy a better life that, I never knew, has happened. That discourse remembers that of communists, but permits populists to gain access to the power peacefully using in their favor the tools of democracy without needing a bloody revolutionary process.

One more, you Arnold, Nick said, please give us your opinion about populism.

Arnold began: There is something that caught always my attention, whose origin I remember it was commented by us when we were studying the French Revolution, it is that terminology used in politics of "Left" and "Right" that now is being applied also to populism, no offense for anybody, but to me that distinction is not only meaningless but dangerous in the mind of people.

To classify people between right and left is to separate and divide the population one against the other, and if is the case that were not enough, avoiding being included in such alternatives, now there are also "centrist" politicians, who in my opinion can be more dangerous by the uncertainty about the direction of their policy that can bend towards one or other side and also because that attitude at the same time of satisfaction and reject to both sectors is a sample of lack of sincerity. In general, Populism use to be catalogued as a leftist movement, but now to degrade a ruler, those who do not like him say that he is a populist of right, what it has no much sense.

When will people be able to understand that the only classification that makes sense in politics and in the life of each individual is that of those who follow the law and those who violate it?

You are right Arnold that distinction between left and right is meaningless.

I going to make now some considerations about populism opened to your comments.

The ground where Populism can grow is Democracy, because populism rests on people and people of any level are only relevant for politicians if they can be used in the elections arena to maintain a democratic shade and get the power in a peaceful manner and without fight, otherwise if the power is grabbed through a revolution, the outcome is different and it will have an authoritarian tint to other countries.

There are rulers who are populists by nature and others that are labeled as such without being it. Those that do not use the typical language that politicians use to the public in their campaigns and expressed them outside of what is permitted to say in politics, are branded, without justification by his opponents and many others as populist.

Some people make a distinction between agrarian and political populism, but I don't agree, we were talking here of the People's Party in the XIX Century whose members were named populists, but that party has nothing to do with the real meaning of the populism of these days.

Populism is just Populism, that is to say, to address a false discourse to the lower income levels of people, presenting the country, usually far from reality, in a disastrous situation and saying that the great business men and rich people are the cause of their situation and how they can improve their life voting for them that are going to save the homeland.

With that kind of discourse Hugo Chavez won the election in Venezuela in the year 2000 and with a mask of democracy he gave the government and the country to the Cuban communism, he took all the agencies of the government, including the three powers and the army establishing an authoritarian regime, continued by his successor that looted the country, leaving it in ruins.

In **Europe** there are several movements branded as populists that go to the XVI Century, but I do not share that opinion neither that of finding in the French Revolution shades of populism. This was not a populist revolution but a revolution of the people that is different.

In fact I do not share that general attribution of the quality of populist to all those politicians that in front of a clear situation of disaster in their country propose a change in the system to save the homeland, contrarily I would say that of the others that prefer abandon or let the country in that downhill, do not show love or interest by their homeland, nevertheless is necessary to consider the circumstances in each case.

In general, is now when it begins to appear populist movements in Europe. Those of old times that were branded as such do not have properly that character, remember the disturbances of peasants in Germany in the XVI Century, that had more a religious tint as well as the English peasants and other workers movements in the XVII Century with a Protestant background.

It was said also that in Germany the Nazi Party in its beginnings during the Weimar Republic, it used populist arguments to mobilize sectors of the middle class that was suffering a very bad moment, in what a clear anti-Marxist purpose was used.

At the end of the XX Century and beginning of the XXI Century, populist movements are found in Italy with Silvio Berlusconi through "Forza Italia" and his allied "Liga Norte", also in Greece with Siriza and in Spain with Pablo Iglesias and his party "Podemos".

In **Latin America** populism appears together with authoritarianism usually hidden under a democratic cover. Populism needs to find the adequate soil of ignorance or deficient level of culture in the mass of people, a democratic system that permits dissatisfied sectors of people to vote, and preferable a bad economic situation in the country or at least some neglect to the lower stratum of people, all of which is easy to find in some countries.

Names like Peron, Kirchner, Chavez, Morales, Ortega, Lula, Correa, Maduro are good representatives but they do not exhaust the list, at side of the typical populists, there are famous leaders and commanders that the new times of democratic atmosphere have almost eliminated. At the time that political phenomenon like the government of the Castro Brothers in Cuba or their associate Maduro in Venezuela survive only thanks to the passivity of the population that prefer to either move to another country or to adopt a conformist attitude, suffering daily abuse, waiting for an act of providence to fix the problem. Of course, that rarely happens.

Is there any question about Populism? Nick asked to the class.

Lora Lord raised her hand and began to talk: From some time ago Populism is being used more and more for abundant sectors of unscrupulous politicians, I was reading and documenting me about the matter and I arrived to the following conclusion that I'm going to present now to see how you and my fellow students think about them.

First: I verified that the opinions expressed by some of the commentators are not neutral opinions but motivated by their political ideology or interest, consequently are biased opinions and therefore opinions without value.

Second: Other authors transform Populism in something of greater prominence in their writings and elaborate a whole pseudo philosophic theory that besides giving to the matter an unwanted relevance, it takes to nowhere or solve nothing, applying the same appellative to different situations that have nothing to do with the real Populism, sometimes to degrade a governor they don't like.

Third: In spite of all the shades that commentators find in Populism, this has a simple meaning: An attempt to attract disaffected layers of the population by showing them a false or exaggerated picture of the situation and promising a change that the own people would be the author.

Fourth: Apart from a possible real crisis that could exist in a country, the success of populists in their predicament, is directly proportional to the social abandon that lower levels of population are.

Lora, your point of view about Populism is interesting. Is there anybody else who wants to comment something?

Albert said: I also see that effectively there is a confusing discourse about Populism, I remember that it was said here that the French Revolution was not a populist movement but a movement of the people, which make me to consider that the term is used without seeing in deep its meaning.

It was commented also about the U.S. People's Party of 1890 whose members were named populists, this was only a terminology matter, because neither the party nor its members were populists in the way that today the term is considered. In that time Southern and other Midwest farmers supported by their unions began to fight by their rights because their farm products, especially fruit were miserably paid while the intermediaries built incredible fortunes, problem that continue now in most countries.

That it is not populism nor can be used as an example of populism, that is just people fighting for their rights. Nowadays Populism is just a way to deceive credulous people.

I agree with you, Nick said, we are going to touch now a topic of great actuality that possibly could be the germ of further alliances: Globalization.

*   *   *

16

Globalization

We call Globalization to the activity developed by several countries to integrate their trade including the exchange of products, technology, capital transactions and investments.

The concept of Globalization as it is now conceived began in the second half of the 20th Century and it was favored as well by the large migrations and by the technical advances, the first of which was television, to promote movements of people

At the beginning of the 20th century, people that were far away from the so called developed countries, even though they could be suffering hardship in their own countries, they remained there passively, waiting for better times.

When television began to spread through the world, that we can estimate around the sixties or seventies and up of the 20th Century, people in the undeveloped world could see how people enjoyed a pleasant life in other countries, with an abundance of things that they could not even imagine to have. This created a dream for millions of people to go there and so migrations little by little exceeded all previous statistics. All these movements were also favored by the improvement in communications, the proliferation of internet and mobile phones.

The share of the elements used for communication began to develop an abundant international trade also based on better and faster ways of transportation, more important in the development of Globalization than in migrations, because people who wanted to reach a promissory country moved through other countries until they find a possibility of getting to their objective.

We can call this kind of Globalization, social or cultural Globalization because it is promoted and managed by the people instead of by the rulers, in contrast with the political Globalization promoted by the government of each country, which includes the guidelines to the economic part of Globalization.

That said, I would like to know your opinions about Globalization, its causes, effects and consequences. Who wants to say something?

Lora Lord began. In spite of what I have read in several articles about the matter, especially in a moment when in several parts of the world people were protesting against Globalization, I don't understand clearly the reason for such protests.

In my opinion Globalization is good or bad depending of the angle we see it. It is good for some countries and bad for others, even more, in the same country it can have a positive and negative impact at the same time, and then we will need to establish the balance between both impacts. Possibly Abu or Frederick as economists could give us a better explanation on this matter finished Lora.

I believe that Globalization is something positive, Abu said and Frederick intervened to express his opinion on the contrary.

Well, Nick said, Abu you first, explain to the class why you consider Globalization positive for a country.

Abu said: I can mention the positive aspects I find in Globalization, but that does not mean that it could have also other negative shades.

Globalization helps develop a closer and friendlier relationship among countries reducing barriers to the import and export of goods and services.

It is very convenient for undeveloped countries that can export to big markets thanks to their low level of costs that allow them to offer lower prices, and this seen from the other end shows that cheap production permits developed countries to buy imported goods at a cheaper price than the local ones, without taking other considerations like the impact on local producers.

Globalization eases trade among countries reducing custom tariffs between countries that not only favor the big importer but also exports of other small merchants of the manufacturing country.

The movement of goods among countries not only increases relations and communication among them but also affects favorably the global economy.

In poor countries where products for developed countries are manufactured, Globalization produces plenty of work and prosperity not only by the sales but also by the knowledge they acquire about technology, through the know-how they receive for the manufacturing process, which otherwise it would be difficult to reach for them, with the advantage that all the activity is a product of their trade activity and free will, not imposed.

Other advantage for the consumers of any country is the availability of worldwide products and through the products a better knowledge of foreign cultures.

As importers must be sure of the quality of the products imported from undeveloped countries, they are paying attention to their ecological system and sanitary conditions.

In those occasions when a big company of a developed country decides to build a factory in an undeveloped country to manufacture their product abroad in a cheaper market, it will produce employment in a country where is very much needed.

Ok, Nick said, now Frederick what do you see of negative in Globalization?

As Abu said, Globalization has positive effects, but the negative aspects that I find are:

When the big companies of a country decide to manufacture their products abroad to get cheaper costs, it will produce an important level of unemployment in their own country, so on one side, the general public will benefit of lower prices with the imported products but for many other people it will mean unemployment.

On the contrary, in the exporting country all will be beneficial, more jobs to the population, large income from exports, learning of new production systems and know-how.

It was said that one of the advantages of Globalization was the free trade among countries by the elimination of import barriers, but this it is not completely true, inside the frame of the agreements signed, each country does its utmost to get some extra benefit through some kind of taxes, to imports or to consume.

In this game of Globalization, the best market is determined by the cost of manufacturing, together with the easiness provided by the government in taxes taking into account how important quantities of production will benefit the country, but not all is beneficial to the exporter country and to the world nature, because the countries chosen usually are not prepared to assume the contamination and pollution that a production of such a level can suppose.

Besides the problems of contamination, are those of the workers that reach almost a slavery status, using even children, about which the importer only has control if it installs its own factory abroad.

The production of merchandise protected by exclusive and expensive trademarks supposes the risk of a proliferation of fake copies of the original products that are being seen all over the world in the streets of any city in detriment of the owners of the original marks and of the merchants legally established that pay their taxes.

I would also add the international movement of people as a damage referred to Globalization, large migrations among countries fade the traditional typical characteristics of the receptor countries, out at the time that contribute to the proliferation of diseases nonexistent before in some areas of the world.

Very well Frederick, Nick approved, let me add some details on the matter.

I think that in a future, that could be not so near, the world in a high percentage will be ruled by only one power, but Globalization as we know it now, can be a problem at long term.

The traditional politics in the United States of equal opportunities, favoring free trade has produced a deterioration of the welfare in the country that comes from the times of the end of the Second WW.

The United States lost its internal car market letting Asia and Europe invade its own market. The proliferation of the global tendency passed by several steps: Japan, Taiwan, Hong Kong, Singapore, South Korea and China besides other minor markets, and the situation became a sort of menace that can change the political structure of the world.

It is enough to see the evolution of China in the past few years to understand the effect of having put technology and know-how in its hands. I have nothing to criticize to China that have done the best use of that opportunity, the reprehensible behavior is that of the EEUU companies (and of many other countries) that thinking only in profits, risked their own future survival.

The political situation in China now, is the best in the world, better than that of Russia and United States because Russia has big internal problems that come from the bankruptcy of the communist system and an unbalance between authoritarianism and democracy that they need to adjust. With respect to the United States, it has the problem of the deficiencies of democracy already commented in this seminar.

In this second decade of the century and onwards they will survive those who know how to defend national interests and not be carried away by the current Globalization that each day has less sense, nevertheless saying that, I do not refer to countries association as the European Union that without doubt is a good step to the unavoidable future although they have to introduce the necessary changes to overcome deficiencies confronted up to now by international organisms as is the case of the United Nations, that affect the good world functioning.

I would want to know if you have any comment or additional question about Globalization.

Rag Kumar raised his hand and said: I agree with you about the political tact that rulers must have nowadays managing politics, even more I would say that in my humble opinion to survive with success at this moment is a hard challenge occasioned by the abundant political opponents of any kind everywhere that disturb and make difficult the task of rulers.

China with a population of 1,387,170,017, approximately 18.47% of the total population of the world, around three times the population of Russia (141,680,935) and the United States (326,056,365) together, represent the best potential market in the world.

It is a fact that products manufactured by china can be found almost in any country of the world, both original products manufactured and exported by order of owners of the trademarks and fake ones of the same products illegally exported usually to Chinese wholesalers in many countries to be retailed by street vendors.

Additionally China develops an intense activity traveling through the world in part for tourism but also expanding its commerce and learning new activities.

If hypothetically China suddenly decides to stop exports of any kind, it will produce a terrible scarcity of merchandises almost impossible of substitute at their prices. China is extending little by little its new welfare to all the population but time still has to pass. What is sure is that with its internal market it can substitute any other.

The new government in U.S. has offered to work for the recovering of the American industrialization and restore its old prestige in the world, but to achieve it the government will have to overcome all public and private interests.

Those that blindly defend Globalization say that it will make the world better and it will avoid poverty and unemployment This is not true because while increase employment in one country, at the same time, it produces unemployment in another, and poverty happens any way.

In conclusion it is clear that the United States is the big loser in this game of Globalization.

I agree with you, Nick said, we are going to touch now a topic related with the effects of Populism but also originated in other ways: The abuse of people.

173

17

The abuse of people

Throughout the history of the world, one important cause of many of the problems faced by humanity has been the thoughtless abuse of people; this has originated riots, wars, revolutions and bloody revenges.

In old times, when people were more obedient under the power of religion and the strength of the powerful, those social explosions were not a matter of simple inconformity but of a great abuse from the strong on the weak, to an extent that with today's mind it is difficult to understand.

At the beginning, the abuse was in the form of invasion and subjugation and, in the evolution of the Roman Civilization we can find great examples that can be an inspiration to the future.

We can mention when Rome invaded Hispania to cut possibilities of supplies to Carthaginians, they found resistance from the several local tribes and proceeded to a general invasion, during which we have two examples against the abuse that deserve to be mentioned.

The first one, it was de city of Numantia, in the vicinity of what is today the Province of Soria, at that time populated by Celtiberians. In the year 153 BC Numantia had the first hostility with Rome, hostilities that continued during 20 years. In 133 BC Rome sent <u>Scipio Aemilianus Africanus</u> with the mission to destroy the city. Scipio the Africanus decided to siege the city, round it with a moat and a well done wood rod fence with towers to strengthen it. The siege lasted 13 months, and when the population, almost dead of starvation, was unable to fight, they decided to burn out the city and to die there free, rather to be slaved.

The other example also in Hispania was the one of Viriatus. Rome had divided Hispania in two halves: Hispania Citerior (the half East) and Hispania Ulterior (the half West) this was in the Hispania Ulterior, in the Lusitania where is now Portugal.

After abundant hostilities between Romans and Lusitanians, these fearing the result of a war with Rome on 152 BC made a peace agreement with the Roman <u>Marcus Atilius</u>, but the terms of the agreement were so hard, that the Lusitanians broke the agreement and attacked several places and recovered part of the loot taken by the Romans. A year later in 151 BC The Praetor of the Hispania Ulterior Servius Sulpicius Galba jointly with Lucius Licinius Lucullus Governor of Hispania Citerior, attacked Lusitania, Galba from the South and Lucullus from the East.

The Lusitanians, unable of resist the two attacks sent emissaries to Galba to negotiate the peace, Galba accepted and a peace treaty was signed with the obligation to the Lusitanians to abandon arms and their homes to live in an open place as well as to be separated in three groups and wait that new land will be given to them, while they were waiting, Galba surrounded them with a trench and his army avoiding any possibility of escape, then Roman soldiers went and executed all men able to fight and sent the survivors to Gaul to be sold as slaves.

The continuous abuse of Romans, made the entire Tribe of Lusitanians mustered of courage and began to fight against Rome but with scarce results. It was then when appeared Viriatus a Lusitanian who was able to survive and escape the massacre to his people and offered himself as leader of the Lusitanians.

Viriatus according to the circumstances, used two kinds of war: "bellum", a normal open fight in the country or "latrocinium", guerrilla attacks inconvenient to Romans that had their formal way of fight. First mention of Viriatus is in 149 BC when with an army of ten thousand invaded Turdetania located in the South of Hispania.

Later on with one thousand men rescued a group of Lusitanians that were under siege from ten thousand Romans. Lusitanians, armed with farm tools defeated the Roman army of Caius Vetilius of ten thousand, killing four thousand including the own Vetilius. After that, Viriatus defeated the Roman army of Gaius Plautius, Gaius Negidius and others.

Responding to those events, Rome sent 15,000 infantry soldiers and 2,000 cavalry commanded by Quintus Fabius Maximus to reinforce the army already existent in Hispania and most of these soldiers were lost fighting against Viriatus. In a new battle Quintus Fabius Maximus was completely defeated.

These events in Hispania together with the other mentioned of Numantia were considered in Rome a problem to solve and Rome sent Quintus Fabius Maximus Servilianus who fell into an ambush by Viriatus, but this instead of harm them let them go.

Maximus Servilianus established a peace agreement with Lusitanians that was ratified by Rome declaring Viriatus "amicus populi Romani". The peace agreement did not please Quintus Servilius commander of the army in Hispania who manifested to Rome that such agreement was dishonorable to Rome. The senate authorized Quintus Servilius to act against Viriatus but in a secret way. Viriatus sent three emissaries to see Quintus Servilius to establish the peace who bribed them and when they returned to the territory of Viriatus killed him while he was sleeping. According commentators of that time (Eutropius), when the killers went to claim the reward offered to them they were answered "Rome does not pay traitors"

What do these two examples mean to you? Nick asked to the class.

The first shows how people can prefer to die rather than being abused, slaved or oppressed in some way, Sarah said, and continued, the second permits us to understand that people were always the same, some clever and others no, some faithful and others traitors and how this existed, exists and will exist for ever. Examples such as these that you mentioned are many in the history of the world. It is the eternal Judas of the Christian Faith.

Thank you Sarah, Nick said, we have seen two reactions of people to the abuse by invasion or domination, now we will give a look to the reaction to the abuse in kingdom and feudal systems, especially in all the Middle Ages.

The study of the way of living in medieval times take us to conclude that the abuse we are considering was everywhere in higher and lower levels, according to the possibilities of impunity each one had. Of course higher class meant more power and more power meant more capacity for unpunished abuse, so the abuse was reflected in all aspects of their daily life.

We have to mention that class named "villain" and the social condition that supposedly existed between a slave and a free man. The abuse on this class had no limits, the villain was attached for life to the land, and he only could leave the land to deliver a message of his Lord or to accompany him to war.

Other custom that produces indignation is the famous "droit du seigneur" in French or "ius primae noctis" in latin, or "right of first night" in English also known as "droit of jambage" in French or "derecho de pernada" in Spanish and other several definitions that exist.

That was the right of the lord to have sexual intercourse with the bride the wedding night before the husband, circumstance that, in some cases could be avoided by giving to the Lord half of the dowry the bride has given.

This extraordinary example of abuse on people is not something new at the time, it was practiced in different moments and places and it can be found as far as in 2000 BC mentioned in "The Epic of Gilgamesh"

Do you have any comments about the abuse on people during the times we commented? Nick asked to the class.

It was Emily who answered. I do not have words to express what I feel hearing such comments.

Well Emily, that's nothing new, Gregory said, we have to agree with the proverb that says that "man is wolf for man" the famous "homo homini lupus" expressed in other words by Plautus in his Asinaria and parodied many times by other authors through history among which Erasmus in his "Adagia", Thomas Hobbes in "De Cive" and Sigmund Freud in his "Civilization and its Discontents" among others. It is not only the abuse of the powerful on the weak because if the weak has the opportunity to associate with others would attack the powerful even in the case of not having received any attack from him.

It is terrible to think that humans could behave as it was said! Emily finished.

Nick intervened. Do you really think that the human being is so bad?

There are many examples and proofs of that. Do you have any proof on the contrary? George commented.

I think so, Nick said, I agree that the information we can see and read everyday coming from the whole world induces us to be pessimist but it is never good to generalize.

Let us suppose you are in an extreme situation and you need money to feed your family and yourself, you know that Emily has in her hand bag twenty thousand dollars and you find her alone and there is not any witness. Would you harm her to get the money you need so much?

Of course not, Gregory said, I would ever do such a thing.

I am safe; any way I do not have that money, Emily said smiling.

You see, Nick said, you are not a wolf to your fellow beings, and as you there are many other people.

Do you think that the behavior can depend on the situation that anyone is living?

No, everybody is as is, usually from birth, who was able to do something wrong or illegal possibly will repeat his action again.

Do you think that justice plays an important role in the behavior of beings?

No, Justice, functions independently of people, but each one depending of his mental structure decides what justice is for him influenced by the circumstances and acts accordingly.

Do you agree with the meaning of Justice from the old Romans?

If you refer, for example, to that of Ulpian of "To give each one his right" Nick said, yes, it was as valid in his time at the beginning of our era as it is today, you as a lawyer know that many of the institutions of the Roman law continue being used in most countries.

That's true, Philip said.

Now, Nick continued, we will make an analysis about the abuse of people in modern and contemporary times and what the future time could be.

I would like to know your comments on when and how a change was produced that made the world to convert the middle age way of thinking into a different one.

Rag asked permission to speak: About how, I think that it was with the Industrial revolution and as to when it happened, it seems that could be in the last half of the XVIII Century. The specific shape as it occurred was the manufacture of cotton's cloth in large quantities and the place of beginning was England.

Now, applying this to our study of people's abuse, I have to add that at that moment, people was abandoning the countryside where they were unable to get the necessary means for living and came to the cities to work in factories where at least they had a fix salary.

That was a moment of real exploitation and abuse of people, who had to work more time than they could bear and worked without distinction: men, women and children.

New inventions and the improvements in the machinery increased the efficiency of the looms that produced more and more and as well, more and more people came to the cities moved by the possibility of working.

Very well Rag, approved Nick, later on, the pressure on workers, led them to unite and soon the unions appeared to defend the rights of workers against their employers. It was a common process: any action (the pressure on workers) produces a reaction (the workers got together to fight) and this takes us to the time we are living through a process that we already commented talking about political systems.

Already for a long time, we are living an atmosphere of freedom favored by the political democratic systems existent in many countries. Are people now free of abuse? What do you think?

No, Lora said, it is not easy for me make a comparison with other times that I only know by reference, but forgetting what happened in the past, let's look at the deficiencies that people are suffering today.

Without needing to see official statistics anybody can be aware by the daily news of what we can call modern slavery, that is to say, people of any age, including small children, recruited by force to fight in wars of so many guerrilla movements in the world. There is also traffic of people to compel them to work as slaves, or for sex activities specially women and children. This is so true that it was a matter of concern to the United Nations in the Palermo Protocol but it does not mean that the problem was solved.

How traffickers do that, goes from the forcible abduction of people to the use of deceivable tools as the social nets in Internet offering, for example, interesting work to young women that are afterwards forced in other country to prostitution, with the only options to obey or die. Similar situations are found in domestic work, more difficult to control to the authorities and also supported by the ignorance and fear of the victims.

In some countries of Southern Asia thousands of people are compelled to work as slaves to pay a debt, even debts of their parents of which the victim of traffickers is not aware.

To end, I consider that Internet that is used by people of all ages besides its utility it is also a dangerous tool as per the constant police actions against child abusers and traffickers detected in the net.

Thank you Lora, now to finish our comments about the abuse of people, let us see what the future holds, although it will be only a advancement of our imagination based on the knowledge and the experience we are living.

Is there somebody that wants to venture something?

Arnold raised his hand and began: Talking about lost of freedom, abuse of people and forced submission, I see a very dark future.

Considering as a fact the human nature and joining it together to the incredible technological advances that improve every day, the bad boys will have the necessary tools to subjugate others and also governments will have a total capacity of control on citizens that they could use according to their need and convenience.

That is enough for today, Nick said, how that future could be is a subject that will be commented in our next class dedicated to the effect of electronics on people.

* * *

18

Electronics, the last slavery

In our last class we have analyzed how people was abused throughout the times, now we are going to focus on something that can subdue people in the future, but that is already beginning as an addiction in millions of people: the electronic world.

In fact, under different forms and uses, electronics has come into our life up to the point that soon it will be impossible to get rid of it.

Mobile phones, video games, digital pictures, videos, computers, tablets, wireless home accessories of any kind, chips for several uses and so on, have captured people of all ages at home, in the street, in the school, in the office; and anywhere you go you will find yourself assisted by electronics, Wi-Fi is today available in all parts in order to help people to use internet or communicate with others.

But this is nothing in comparison with what will come, now credit cards have a chip that includes users data, in some countries the

Social Security card has a chip that shows doctors of any center you go, all your clinical history, which permits doctors to help you easier and ensures you a better assistance.

In a possibly not so distant future, a chip could be inserted inside us with all our public data as a way of identification, accessible to public offices, police and immigration departments that will show our presence if we pass near any of the many control detectors of the State, in fact I have heard recently in the news about a Scandinavian enterprise that is inserting a tiny chip in the hand of his employees for access and identification.

When that moment arrives, the control on citizens will be total. Assuming a fair government it will not be important for those who abide by the rules of their community, but criminals will be better controlled although, as today happens, with all certainty, they will invent ways of circumventing such controls.

Please, let me know your opinion about that hypothetic, but predictable situation.

The first to speak was Sarah Morrison.

I understand that the evolution we are seeing now and at such a fast pace, makes it feasible that outcome. What comes to my mind is a sort of paradoxical situation: human beings are each time more similar to the machines and on the other hand, machines are each time more similar to human beings.

I think, if a devastating war does not occur before, in about ten or twenty years time, robots will be so common as computers, in the same way, medicine will advance in a marvelous way, the question is however: Will it be better or worse for people?

Lora Lord intervened: I fully understand your concern and you are right. I believe that such situation will be seen as natural by the new born people of that time, because it will be their life and they will consider us as images of a museum. It looks a sad outcome.

Now Gregory spoke. We, philosophers see things in a different way; we go directly to the mind of people to find the ultimate causes of what is happening.

The target of our work is the mind, interrupted Sarah, we the psychologist investigate why and how the mind conditions and rules our daily life.

Yes, Gregory said, but your study throughout the mind is addressed to analyze and try to understand the human behavior, what would you say about the actions of a robot?

We have nothing to do with machines, our object of study are humans, answered Sarah.

Rag Kumar that had been hearing the opinions of his fellow students said: I am afraid Sarah that I cannot agree with you, I understand that from a traditional point of view you are right, but Psychology needs to update the scope of its study. Let me explain, robots, and more every day, are not simple machines, scientists are working hard to achieve that robots could interact with human beings helping them; and even, and this is more important, protecting them. For that purpose the programming of a robot that is supposed to act between people with the ability of understand them and to take immediate decisions to unexpected and possibly dangerous situations, must include the capacity of making an instant analysis of its environment and take an action based on justice, taking even into account moral values and decide what is the correct action between two, which possibly none of them are good.

For that purpose, if a robot is able to see and perceive what is happening in its environment and it's required that adopt decisions, it needs to have a sort of mind that it will be in one of its memories containing the basic principles of justice that will be provided by the programmer who it will be the inspiration of the mind of the robot in the same way that the inspiration of our mind possibly comes from a spiritual world.

In conclusion, when robots reach to such a high development their "mind" could be analyzed although that analysis will show the characteristics of the mind of the programmer or programmers, but if the program is well conceived it will include moral values, and justice reasons for acting and consequently liable of being influenced by the words of a psychologist or someone with a good capacity of reasoning.

It is a point of view, Sarah accepted, it is possible that we have to confront soon that kind of situations.

Nick added: our point of interest is not so much the way how robots can reason under their programming but the use that governments, or some unscrupulous people, can do of them and of technology to subdue people or for warlike purposes. In my opinion, the good or bad will be in the quality of those who control the robot.

Arnold intervened to say: Supposing that a government will not make a bad use of the information about citizens, if we are talking of millions of people not even will be looking at the data of an individual unless there is a reason such as a criminal or illegal action of the individual and in this case is good to have an efficient control to stop actions that can damage the community.

I do not agree with you, Barbara said, privacy must be respected; anywhere you go, there is a camera recording what people do, to me that's not fair.

Why not? Cameras are in public areas to protect people, if a burglar or a killer acts against people, recordings will permit identify the criminals, stop them, and avoid further damage to the community.

It would be different if the cameras were in your home, that would be a violation to your privacy, but who is in a public area must understand that is exposed to public observation of people around him, cameras and so on, although not to use private cameras to put your image in a social net or the like, this is what is not permitted.

Well, Nick said, then, in your opinion could electronics be an instrument to subdue people?

Yes, it could be. They agree almost unanimously.

Drawing conclusions

19

The urgency of an effective Supranational Central Organism

After greeting the class, Nick began: This will be our penultimate class, this and next class will be dedicated to something of vital importance if we want to continue enjoying the relative world peace we had since around seventy years ago and to which we were referring in former classes.

There were some events that were big and terrible events to those who suffer them as it was, and continues being, several kinds of terrorism, but not a generalized war with the terrible effects that could have if we think in the devastation power of modern weapons.

This was precisely what keep the peace, in spite of the stupid and rapacious minds of many politicians, the fear to a new war, that is to say, we enjoyed a peace based on the strength of the principal countries of the world.

We are facing two well defined alternatives: its own interest, that is to say, a country, any country, can protect itself to the extent of its possibilities establishing all necessary means for its own security, but if it does not feel enough strong, to be secure, it can look for the association with other powerful countries to keep the world safe.

Which of these two alternatives is the right one? Of course the one that looks for the general interest, because own protection it is all right but not enough in front of the general power unless the country considers itself more powerful than the rest of the world.

Thinking consciously and taking into account the human nature, is easy to arrive to the conclusion that peace it is not the result of good desires, at side of this is necessary also strength. The world is populated by good and bad people, when bad people get power other people have to be prepared to resist or counteract their actions otherwise will be subdued or even slaved.

Nick addressed to the class. What does slavery mean for you?

Emily answered. To be captured and used as a thing for any purpose for free and for ever.

Your concept about slavery is true but has more to do with the old times, Nick said, today the concept, as many other things, has evolved, even though people of all ages continue being kidnapped to be used in war in underdeveloped areas of Africa, Middle East, Asia and South America.

There are countries subdued by political abuse of their rulers, as is the case of Cuba and Venezuela kidnapped by more than sixty and seventeen years respectively and several other countries in similar situation under the camouflage of democracy or unpredictable rulers without any respect to the world community of which they are part as is the case of, for example, North Korea.

Many people was captured by Islam terrorism and war movements of several countries in Africa or the Colombian guerrilla where men were forced to struggle and women to struggle and to sexual abuse for many years.

Rag raised his hand; Nick authorized him to talk and said: precisely it was just signed an agreement between the government in Colombia and the FARC main guerrilla movement and they are now in negotiations with the ELN to make a similar agreement, by which the guerrilla has to give up their armament, join the civil life and integrate into the political system. Do you think that this is something positive for Colombia?

I prefer to have your opinion, Nick said, you that puts the topic on the table, what do you think?

Rag Kumar answered: I really wanted to know your opinion to compare it with what I think at this respect, which is as follow: we are talking of a guerrilla group that during many years has kidnapped and killed a huge number of people, men, women and children were compelled to fight as soldiers, (it has been estimated that at least a quarter of the forces of the guerrilla are minors) women besides being part of their army were used as sexual slaves for the soldiers.

Their main source of financing was in one or other form drug trafficking that it was estimated, reached yearly many billions of US dollars, but they also used the extortion to drug planters or other farms, at the time, they robbed banks and all kind of atrocities in small groups of country houses inside the country.

I could continue in a large enumeration of acts against people, public and private property in which the life of their Colombian compatriots had not any value.

And now my opinion is that I find immoral, absolutely unfair and a terrible example to the world, an agreement by which from one day to the other, the people of that criminal organization pass to be among the other citizens, without punishment for their killings, robberies and kidnappings.

The only description I can find to the president of Colombia, author of such agreement is that he doesn't know or are not interested in the meaning of justice or it is possible that he cannot reason normally, in any of such cases he wouldn't be directing the destiny of a country, because he handed Colombia over to a group of terrorists. What is your opinion professor?

I think you are right, the president of Colombia argued that it was more important to finish with that guerrilla war, but that has to be done with the country army, of course, unless that the Colombian army is inferior to an internal guerrilla group.

Is there anybody else who wanted to make any comment about this?

Sara Morrison intervened: I have followed occasionally the evolution of this process that is in the news since 2012 and I cannot believe how they can be inserted into civilian life without the correspondent punishment. Criminals that besides killing the population, kidnapped women that were raped and forced to abort, without mentioning children of both genders made into soldiers. This agreement only means the abandonment of the country in a short term to those criminals and the punishment they would deserve must be applied also to President Santos who will be the only responsible of the destiny of his country and instead of being praised he will be cursed by history.

In our time who knows! Albert said, by now he was awarded, for that, the Nobel Price.

That means nothing, Abu argued, already several people rejected the price, except in science, I think that the selection they do is deficient or biased.

Well, Nick interrupted, now we will continue saying that all those situations that we were commenting are ways of slavering, modern slavery, but slavery all the same. Each time the mind of people is forced to do something contrary to their own will we are before a kind of slavery. If a husband abuses physical or mentally of his wife or sons, that is slavery. This was, is, and it will be. The challenge to the mind is to know if it is possible to overcome such situation and if it is feasible to find a solution.

Referring to countries, under the postulates of the International Law, there are abundant bilateral and multilateral treaties that are in force, which sometimes are complied with and sometimes are not. The frictions between countries are constant, even in the time we are living there are countries invading and conquering territory of other countries, the commented fact of men and children kidnapped and forced to fight in war and women to satisfy terrorists, is something that seems unbelievable but is true.

History showed us that a permanent peace is almost impossible and when it occurs is remembered as something unheard of, as is the case, already commented, of the Pax Romana (Roman Peace) that lasted 206 years, from 27 BC to 180 AD, also known as Pax Augusta because it was set up in the Roman Empire by Augustus.

It is appropriate to say in support of our statement that a country has to be permanently strong in peace times, because the inactivity weakens. After the large and peaceful Roman Peace, The Roman Empire, the strongest empire ever existed asleep on its laurels was defeated by the barbarian tribes.

Now in our time after the end of the Second World War, the world has been enjoying a period of partial peace that has lasted already for 70 years and now is in the threshold of a new conflagration.

What are the points of rupture? More than necessary:

Iran, attempting to made itself powerful e-nough through nuclear weapons, a danger to the area and to the world.

Syria, a country in war for years, with all its physical structure destroyed continues its conflict and could be a danger to the peace by the competing interest involved.

Israel and Palestine have been for many years in a sort of fight, unbalancing the peace of the area as the result of something done in a wrong way, and things badly done cannot produce a good result. People in the world cannot understand why is denied to Palestinians the right of being a State. It is said that they don't want to recognize the State of Israel, possibly because they were removed from there to put the new created Israel State, but this has nothing to do with their recognition as a State. Perhaps the small but powerful Israel can say something about that. Iraq, where people dies almost every day in terrorist explosions as a consequence of a war promoted using a false pretext and involving deceptively the help of other countries. Only from U.S. 4,498 soldiers were killed and 32,249 wounded in this war apart of those killed or wounded from U.S. Allies and Iraqi forces to a total of around 35,000 people dead. And all that by an error or a whim!

The Ukrainian crisis that comes since 2013, is confronting Russia and the European Union by the Russian annexation of Crimea, in 2014 and the war between the Ukrainian government and the insurgents in favor of Russia, supported by Russian forces.

North Korea since 2011 ruled by Kim Jong-Un, it has become a menace to the world by its constant threats, that made South Korea and Japan to feel insecure, additionally there are the North Korea research and experiments to achieve rockets able to reach U.S. territory. The problem was discussed in the United Nations but the question is: what has to be done, expect an attack and answer it or prevent it?

Other points of rupture come from political pseudo communists tendencies materialized in what is being named populist parties governing or trying to govern, profiting the easiness of the democratic voting system.

All what they need to do is to flatter the lowest levels of the population, that they know very well how to do it, with all kind of possible and impossible offers, creating a dream in ignorant people, from which they will wake up when the demagogues reach the power, but then it will be too late and the remedy will be difficult.

How to avoid all that potential danger that is menacing the world is easy of deducting, it is necessary an international organism well structured, supported by the most powerful countries of the world, with the purpose of maintaining peace permanently among them and to prevent and correct the abuse on people in any place, no matter if the country is a member or not of the organism, because a situation of disaster in any place, can be a symptom of unbalance to the world that it will need to be remedied.

Do not say to me that the organism already exist making reference to the United Nations, because the UN has nothing to do with what we are talking, such organism must be in capacity of acting and intervene in any country guilty of producing an international friction or of internal abuse to its citizens and restoring it to a normal situation.

The situation in the UN depends of the most powerful States as well of those small ones that support them or are associated with others with common political interest, even if acting criminally.

The UN cannot solve any problem with its current configuration; the terms of the constitution of an adequate organism must establish its rights and way of action, which have to be above the opinion of a specific country and of course must have an army capable of defeating any transgressor country separately.

I do not need to say that the creation of a such organism will be complex by the different interest of the states, but that can be solved if the organism is not ruled by a single person but by an assembly of several consultants of different countries, whose decisions, based in fair bylaws, approved by a majority of votes are decisive.

This, together with the good desire of peace of the parts will be enough to have peace and stability on the world. My dear friends, I am not talking for those that say "this is very difficult" or "impossible" for that people all doors are always closed, they are the one who in advance accept to be subdued.

Is there any observation? Nick asked.

The students look at each other and finally Lora Lord said: Professor, I think I dare not to say anything because you can think that I am one of that kind of people you just said, any way I go to express my opinion.

First of all, I agree with you because everybody can see in the daily news permanent information about all kinds of abuses from a country to another country and from a country on its citizens, that is to say, we see how who has power abuses on the weak, according with its convenience.

It goes without saying that if a powerful organism exists, empowered by the states of the world taking care of the right functioning of the international community, avoiding unfair situations in a country or between countries, well controlled, without possibilities of any kind of corruption among its representatives, it will be a golden dream to the world.

Philip raised his hand and asked: How would you prevent the corruption in such an organism?

With good internal elements of control, to avoid that if something wrong happens it couldn't remain hidden and is discovered immediately; and also to avoid proliferation of any kind of corruption, the maximum punishment to infractions; all public servants will know from the beginning what they are risking if they act illegally or criminally and consequently if they are not thinking to act illegally there is not reason to reject the position and the punishment is justified and cannot be discussed, not even by the own officials in charge that accepted the kind of punishment when they assumed the position.

Now was Rag Kumar who made a question.

With so many countries involved and a different way of seeing things, the decisions of the Assembly will unavoidably produce frequent conflicts with the country that believes that it has been injured. It will oppose strongly a decision and its unconformity will be a germ of disagreement. How can this be solved?

Nick answered: if the decisions of the respecttive justice agency, that as the Assembly it will be integrated by several members, are fair and based in evidence that cannot be questioned, the country in question has not other option than to accept the verdict.

Now George asked: Are you sure that all possible failures could be taking into account in advance to avoid further discussions among members?

Absolutely, Nick answered, if things are well done from the beginning and all possible situations are considered, there will not be problems in the future.

Arnold Man intervened, I completely agree with you, because as a lawyer I work for my clients in that way and I always take all the responsibility for what I do.

Our time is over, Nick said, we will continue in our next and final class with this comments about a possible world control to maintain peace.

20

A World Confederation

Today in the last class of this seminar, we are going to talk about something that only a small group of people is thinking about or believing in, something that can be a solution or a final danger, according to how is structured from the beginning: A total supranational community, or said in other words, a World Confederation.

The failures in the majority of the international treaties are the concessions made to the parts in its creation to satisfy their interests. That cannot exist in the creation of a World Community, the only interest that can be considered is that of the participating countries, I even would suggest a slogan like "Good for one, good for all" If people know that every one is the same as the others, they will trust and will be calm.

Of course, taking into account the human nature, although the countries have accepted the conditions to become members, it is possible that after a while, some of them would want to abandon the community, circumstance that must be foreseen and completely regulated from the very beginning.

Do you think that I consider the creation of a world Community integrated by all the states of the planet as something easy? No, on the contrary, I know that it is a hard but not an impossible task. It is not necessary that all countries ratify the initial agreement, something around a half of the world population will be enough to begin, provided the most powerful countries belong to it; the success and the power of the coalition, together with the advantages of being part of the community will be sufficient motivation to the others.

If such a coalition is proposed, for sure some countries will be reluctant to the idea, it is for that reason that it is not enough to talk about the project, all documents containing the complete structure of the new community will have to be prepared, explaining what will be the effect on the countries by their adhesion to the community and all the advantages of belonging to it.

No country will desire to be affected in its internal order and functioning and it won't happen, each country will keep its own organization as before, including its army, particular administration and its political system with its usual elections, which cannot be contrary to the regulations of the community. The adhesion to the community must be decided by the population of each country voting in their usual way and ratified after in a referendum, supervised by representatives of the community to warrant its impartiality.

After the beginning of the first conversations on this matter all the population of the world will be cognizant of the purpose and ways of functioning of the community, as well as the advantages of being a member, both, for the country and for each individual citizen.

What will be the pitfalls that will undoubtedly arise? Can you imagine something?

Rag Kumar began; to answer that, I would need to have a good idea of what will be presented to the countries, but as of now I guess politicians could be a first obstacle, fearful of being affected in their personal interests and of course we would have to count with protest demonstrations against the project in several places of the world, promoted for those who consider the project against their interests and others that were paid for that.

Also, the most powerful nations will attempt to impose their will and modify the project at their convenience and also the leaders of small almost unknown countries could be reluctant, thinking that for them is better to be the head of a mouse rather than the tail of a lion.

I think that the advantages of being member must be clearly highlighted.

Your opinion has a logic base, Nick said, and then addressing to the class: As every thing has advantages and disadvantages, I would like to know your opinion on the advantages and disadvantages of the existence of a well structured World community and to the countries to be part of it.

To answer, do not think in the two attempts we have in history as are the " The Society of Nations" and "The United Nations" because what we are proposing now it has nothing to do with them or have any similarity, in any case, it has more similarity with the founding of the European Union.

Arnold Man raised his hand and said: Before talking about the advantages of something is necessary to know what that something is, so beginning by the basics I suppose we are talking of an association of countries under a sort of bylaws that establish the rights and duties of each one of the members.

I think some of the duties can be:

1) Contribution to the maintenance of the community proportionally to the capacity and characteristics of each nation, provided the nation is using fairly its possibilities, otherwise the community could help to a better rational use of its material resources, this obligation will be the same to all members according their possibilities.

2) The obligation to accept the decisions of the Assembly of the community.

3) Contribute with people to the community army in the way that is established.

4) Participate in technological investigations of the community with qualified professionals.

5) Each country member has to develop a good internal administration to achieve the best internal results, which will be indirectly favorable for the community.

I guess there will be many others that must be determined a priory and not later on.

Now we can see the rights and benefits for any member.

1) The first right and benefit for a country is to be part of such a great community, which will mean for the citizens of the country to be also citizens to the whole community.

2) The citizens of any country member will have an electronic identification showing that they are citizens of the community through their country of origin, that is to say, they will have a sort of double nationality while their country is a member of the community.

3) A total protection, help and assistance of the community in any emergency in a country member, which means that any unjustified damage against a country member will be considered damage to the community.

4) Monetary and professional assistance to the country members in any economic emergency, provided they did not originate the problem.

5) Unified programming of production in the whole community, namely production and consume coordinated, which means that any person will have at its disposal any products, natural or manufactured even though they are not produced or manufactured in his country.

6) An attempt to finish poverty looking at the social and personal causes, providing housing and work when needed and in the cases of reluctance of a person to work or to live as the other people, applying the necessary correctives through the affected country.

Nowadays in any country of the world, I dare to say without exception, there are people living in the street or in poor marginal areas where burglars and drugs are abundant, that cannot exist in the cities of the new times.

Well, this it is not something that can be projected in a class in a couple of minutes, I think that it should be the subject of a comprehensive study considering all kind of possibilities and situations. If something is well done from the beginning it will produce good results.

You are right, Nick said. We are talking of something that although it may seem as unlikely or impossible, deserves to be studied because it can mean the salvation of a civilization, for that reason I want to insist on the matter and before continuing I want to know, without going into details of functioning, your opinion if such a project, independently is feasible or not, could be good for the stability of the world. Please only those who consider the project senseless and the reasons why they think so.

Rag Kumar said:

I do not say that such a project has no sense, this idea, from a logical point of view, is bright and must be a solution, but in my opinion unfortunately it won't be, precisely because of the human nature and not for the nature or quality of the project.

Let's suppose the project works and becomes a reality, it will begin a peace and welfare time to the world, the community would be each time stronger thanks to a good and rational administration managed by the Assembly of Nations, the common investigation will increase the discoveries and technological advances, projects that are being considered to be a reality in twenty years could be reality in a few years, but I wonder, if it would not be possible for this community, with the strength gained, constitute itself in a world dictatorship?

Almost everything is possible in life, Nick said, all is a matter of an adequate initial organization and a strict control in the follow up, we are talking of a world organization or almost, and a question that comes instantly to the mind is: where will it be located?

This community cannot have its headquarters in a building but in an international and neutral territory that will have to be chosen by all the country members among the several places the members could offer, this place could be projected according a new futuristic configuration avoiding all the inconveniences of the great cities and it will be a place of maximum security, I guess you are not imagining a city full of cars spreading smoke everywhere. The electronic system of communication used inside the area will be different of the one used in the world, not accessible through internet or other existent net.

This place will have several locations with enough separation between them to accommodate the various departments of the community:

A first main department of that community of countries will accommodate the Headquarters of the assembly and all communication and administrative Departments.

A second department could be the center of specialization where the best students of all countries will reach the highest level in their field of study.

It will have also a center of Security and defense, destined to keep safe the area and the whole community and it will be in contact with the departments of defense of each country member. This department would include the investigation of new more, effective but less invasive weapons and a place to accommodate army forces including robots area, a port and an airport prepared also for interplanetary activity.

A center to manage the productivity of the community with all necessary means to coordinate production and consumption in the world, establishing international prices for all products, sending the excess of production of the countries to those others without production, that need them, trying to balance production and consume in the whole world.

A health center destined to investigate with the collaboration of the best specialists of all countries how to fight illness and promote health in the world.

An aerospace department in the community to improve designs and built new aerial devices.

A vacations center to be used by all the residents of the community headquarters in the established vacations time of each one.

No alien to a department can come into its area without being detected by the electronic controls installed in people and in every department. If someone for any reason has to go to other department he will have to identify himself at the entrance and to obtain the correspondent temporal permission.

Is there somebody else with a comment about why this project cannot work?

Barbara said: The project is great, I believe in it but I think the problem will be to put in agreement the several nations; I refer mainly to the big nations, not for deficiency of the project but for lack of love of politicians to their countries, independently of what they could say. In the same way I think that other obstacle will be the several religions that will attempt to coerce the population according with their respective convenience.

May be you are right, but I dare to say that if we continue in the world as is with all this confrontation of interest, religion fanaticism, arrogant politicians menacing other nations, countries seizing new territories, terrorist attacks here and there and countries dying of hunger, while their governors get rich without measure, in any moment there will be some sort of social explosion or war and the outcome will be terrible.

Well, we have arrived to the end of this seminar; I hope that our interchange of opinions could bc profitable for you in your life and eventually to the world society.

Barbara raised her hand, Nick saw her and said: Yes?

Excuse me professor, if you don't mind I want to remind you about your promise to inform us about the reason of the name of this seminar: *"the myth of politics"*

Nick smiled and said: you are right and I apologize, I had completely forgotten.

I understand your curiosity about why politics was qualified as a "myth" I will try to explain it as best as possible.

21

El Myth of Politics

If you remember the stages we have gone through in this seminar, with reference to the several empires before our era, as well as the further analysis of the several political systems, you will find some elements that getting rid of the political field are always present, and they are:

1. Collectivities of People in which several nationalities or ethnic groups can co-exist.

2. A space of territory occupied by such collectivities.

3. A disparity of criteria about behavior, and preferences among collectivity members.

4. A different quality among the individuals of the collectivity: clever people, individuals with slow response, good workers, individuals reluctant to do any work and individuals interested only in having fun.

5. The people that integrate the community have to feed them, cover their other necessities and live together.

The people that integrate any of those communities have to co-exist together on a daily basis; and taking into account the characteristics of the human nature we have highlighted, it will produce unavoidable conflicts, because we have people with a sense of justice that respect their fellow neighbors, living together with others who let them be taken by their own caprices and attempt to impose their criteria to the rest of population.

This, due to the human nature, always was, is and will be this way; for that reason, as we have seen here, since antiquity, we find reflected in the first laws, provisions against the same crimes that exist in our almost interplanetary times.

So we see that the way how it was attempted to offset deficiencies in the human behavior was throughout rules establishing sanctions and punishments to each kind of crime, the punishment depended of the characteristics of the crime committed, and it could be a pecuniary sanction, a corporal punishment or even death.

The rules regulating the community life were issued by the ruler and usually were based in equity; remember, as an example, the mythic famous judgment of Salomon.

With the passage of time the communities were much larger and it was producing a phenomenon that is normal, that is to say, increased the abuse of the rulers, because at the end, these were people as the others although in certain occasions, they arrogated to themselves or was granted to them a divine character.

In our times the circumstances, although in a larger scale, are the same: people who act out of the frame of justice or against the establishment, make them worthy of the corresponding punishment.

Then, what is politics? Politics, forgetting now etymology and the paraphernalia created by the same politicians, is only the name given to the whole structure that handle the State affaires. But, does politics have a real practical meaning? No, except for the same politicians who adopt politics as a way of life and of course also to the State, while the citizens suffer the deterioration caused by those politicians who are named so only by their field of dedication.

Politics seen from this angle is only an empty shell without substance, a myth! That people have acccptcd by ignorance and repetition, by a reiteration of centuries.

Now I would appreciate your arguments demonstrating the sense of that enormous scheme that in some countries reach hundreds of thousands of people, whom we call politicians and to their activity, politics.

At first there was not any reaction among the students and Nick insisted.

Let's go, you are well capable for that analysis, we pretend to establish if politics as an abstract being has a sense or simply what it contains can subsist without all that structural paraphernalia that politicians organize with the more or less large support of interested sectors of the population.

The question is: Does the State will continue functioning if the so called political class will not exist?

Of course yes, George said, the ruler could designate the most adequate citizens for each department or function, bureaucracy will be enormously reduced and each public worker would act in defense of the homeland and not for a political party or for a political tendency that could be acceptable but also harmful.

Then for you, it would be possible to get rid of the political class as a fact institution? Then, how do you promote a new governor?

Regarding that, in my opinion, we have to distinguish between two kinds of communities: Traditional or primitive communities and new futuristic communities.

In the new futuristic communities, simply by the direct vote of all citizens.

But, which are that futuristic communities for you? Nick asked.

Those that will have to be established if the current game of politics can be discarded, that is to say, communities where the citizens are proud of belonging to them and collaborate to the functioning of the State without thinking in getting a profit from such activity but by love and as a duty to the homeland.

States protected of external contamination and in capacity of facing any external attack, where ignorance and poverty will be eradicated.

Referring to the traditional communities, with all the unfavorable elements, that everyone knows, the situation is more complex by the diversity of levels and degree of preparation of the individuals.

The problem consist in solving the effect of demagoguery on the more ignorant and disadvantaged classes, object of constant fraudulent machinations for their political value, as each one of these citizens means a vote.

How do you propose to solve that? Nick asked.

Without desiring to look pessimistic, George said, in the actual circumstances there is no remedy, because society was structured by politicians at their convenience and guidelines were established and rights granted, which even though could be inconvenient and even dangerous to the functioning of the State, under the actual circumstances are unavoidable.

Then, Nick said, in your opinion does the actual political establishment have no remedy?

Well, continued George, everything in life can have a remedy, the difficulty is to achieve the remedy that is accepted by the collectivity, in this case the elimination of past demagogic concessions only could be achieved using strength, which won't be accepted and would have to be imposed.

What is for you the base of the problem? Nick asked.

The problem lies in a badly understood concept of liberty, perhaps, since almost a century, we could say all over the world, by reasons of political convenience people were being prepared mentally of their right to be free in any sense, but it was omitted to talk about its limits and to specify what it was not considered convenient for political purposes, that is to say, it was omitted to say in what the liberty to which all of us have right consists.

And, in what consists according with you?

In the fact that liberty it is not unlimited, otherwise liberty becomes an instrument of abuse on the other people, letting liberty being and transform itself in licentiousness. It was omitted to clarify, although it has to be clear to anybody thinking right, that the liberty of any member of a community of people forming a State, only can be exercised inside the limits that the law and the rights of the others fellow citizens permits.

That is correct, Nick approved, all actions of the members of a State have to be realized inside the frame of the law and the violations to what the law establishes must be proportionally punished.

In that way, Nick continued, all the stability of the functioning of a State must consist in the existence of a legal system based on equity, hard punishments for its violation and a fair judgment to transgressors, without distinctions or privileges of any kind. That is, simply, the basis for the good functioning of any State, regarding to politics as now we know it is only a myth, an empty shell where we can only find corruption, privileges and abuse of the strong on the weak.

Gentlemen, this seminar is over, I don't know if I will meet you again, you are good thinkers and I hope you use that capacity of reasoning in your respective activities. I do not consider myself your professor but you fellow student, if you need me you know my E-Mail. Good Luck!

All the students stood up and applauded him.

*   *   *

Appendixes

Brief review on the great empires of the antiquity

Summer

In the frame of our knowledge of the antiquity, perhaps we can say that anxiety by the order that the law represents, begins in Summer, south of Mesopotamia, (nowadays Southern Iraq) around the 3500 BC. Possibly it began in the city of Uruk. Sumer was formed by several cities that we can call city-states because though they were part of the whole represented by Sumer each city had its own Government and laws that we can call the Sumerian Law.

Famous characters appeared in Sumer as Gilgamesh a little between fantasy and reality; it is supposed that he was a king of Uruk who reigned in the first half of the third millennia for more than one hundred years.

Gilgamesh, it was said, that he was two thirds god and one third human and is the character of the epic of his name "The epic of

Gilgamesh" that narrates his life and his relation with the gods.

In this period of the Sumerian civilization, they had a theocratic government where the ruler (Ensi) was a priest-king and as it was common at that time the king was assisted by an assembly of elders of both genres (this is an important detail taking into account how later on, women were separated from most functions of the social and religious life)

At this time life was mostly calm, further invasions suggested to build walls around the cities and to have soldiers to defend them.

The oldest Codes of laws known in the world appeared also in Sumer and were written in Sumerian. The law code of Ur-Nammu with the laws of the city of Eshnunna, it seems to be the oldest known (2112-2095 BC) around more than a 300 years before of the world famous Code of Hammurabi.

The Ur-Nammu Code includes humanitarian dispositions protecting orphans, widows and poor people as well as other affecting the daily life of people as equity dispositions about the use of land, condemns for malediction, violence and fights events and regulations on weight system. It establishes punishment to killers, robbers, kidnappers, adultery, divorce, sorcery, false witnesses and others.

Akkadian Empire
Laws of Eshnunna

Sumer was conquered by the **Akkadian empire**, whose center of influence and operations was the city of Akkad. A great empire flourished that united Akkadian and Sumerian cultures during one hundred years, approximately since 2300 BC to 2200 BC, but the Sumerian language prevailed for some uses.

The founder of the new empire was Sargon I of Akkad (2334–2279 BC) whose origin lies between legend and truth and it is not the case to talk about it here. The fact is that Sargon had a long life during which he had the ability of keeping his conquests and maintain his empire, even when being in his old age he suffered several revolts that he defeated at the forefront of his armies.

The Akkadian Empire united Akkad and Sumer equivalent territories to the modern: Iraq, Kuwait, part of Syria, Turkey, Anatolia, Iran and Lebanon.

After the death of Sargon, his two sons reigned successively but briefly as they were assassinated by their own guards. It was his grandson Naram-Sin who returned the glory and even enlarged the empire.

During the first moments of the empire, the monarchy was influenced and even subordinated to religion but this situation was changing to give the king more independence of religion. With Naram-Sin, the king got a divine consideration that in old times only happened after his death.

Since the time of Sargon and afterwards, with Naram-Sin, to maintain the control of the political organization in the territories, the king designed his sons as governors (Ensi) of the provinces and his daughters as high priestess of Sin (the moon deity named Nanna in Sumer) or occasionally made his daughters married with the foreign rulers of new territories.

As is even today, politics was very much influenced by the economic situation of the country. In those times the main source of wealth in a country was agriculture and commerce and the Akkadian Empire had very well irrigated lands thanks to both rivers (Tigris and Euphrates) that crossed the territory and had at that time a large flow of water.

The abundance of water was decreasing while at the same time increased its salinity, which in the last period of the empire was compounded with a substantial change of climate, reduced at a minimum the productivity of agriculture, produced a great scarcity of food and was one of the factors for the fall of the empire.

On the other hand, even in the moments of best agricultural productivity, Akkad lacked all other products that had to be imported, which produced an economical unbalance that was compensated with the conquest of new richer territories.

* * *

Another important legal body besides the commented Ur-Nammu Code was the **Laws of Eshnunna,** a city in the North of Ur on the Diyala river tributary of the Tigris River that got relevance after the fall of Ur. They were found in two tablets (A and B) written in Akkadian that were copies of the original estimated somewhere before the 1900 BC and possibly issued by Bilalama ruler of the city.

The laws of Eshnunna are very similar to the Code of Hammurabi though they were made around two generation before.

Babylon
Hammurabi Code

Three hundred years after the fall of the Akkadian Empire, Babylon flourished as a new empire, The Babylonian Empire with its capital in Babylon lasted from 1900 BC to 1600 BC. Nevertheless several sources seem to indicate that Babylon was founded in the 23rd Century BC. About the founder there are discrepancies.

Later on, from 609 to 539 BC Babylon was the capital of the Neo Babylonian Chaldean Empire. At that time the Hanging Gardens of Babylon were one of the seven wonders of the antiquity though there is not a certainty about where they were located.

After these two moments of glory, Babylon was dominated successively by other civilizations and finally Babylon was ruled by Rome and the Sassanid Empire. During its moments of brightness Babylon was one of the largest cities in the world with a population above the 200,000 citizens.

Its original name was Babilli, from Akkadian terminology that it seems refers to the name of a place where it was located (perhaps Bawer). Later on its name changed to Babili from "Bāb-ili" "Gate of God" that in Aramaic was "Bab-El" "Gate of God" which produced the Babel we can read in the Bible, where in Genesis was interpreted erroneously using the verb "bilbél" "Confusion" to allude the confusion of languages, ordered by God against the people who was building a Tower to reach His world.

The original founding of Babylon is controversial though a majority agrees that it was approximately in the twenty third century BC, and possibly its first king was Belus, while in the Bible in the Book of Genesis it mentions as founder the king Nimrod. Any way, Babylon had not preponderancy in the area until the reign of Hammurabi (1792 bC-1750 BC) the sixth Babylonian king who conquered most of the cities in the South of Mesopotamia, among them: Eshnunna, Lagash, Nippur, Uruk, Ur, Larsa, Isin, Eridu and others, to deserve to be called an empire.

Hammurabi changed not only the appearance of the city but also organized the internal administration of the government, established taxation and expanded Babylonian dominium to all South of Mesopotamia eliminating the Elamite permanent disturbance and brought stability to all the area.

After the death of Hammurabi the empire began its decadency and was dominated by

Assyrian, Kassite and Elamite. Except in the time of Hammurabi, Babylon never was a strong country and it was in some way dominated by successive invaders.

The presence of Hammurabi in Mesopotamia shows how a governor, according to the honesty and efficiency of his rules can change the life of a community.

Besides, it is necessary to mention the **Hammurabi Code** a very well preserved code of around 1754 BC issued by Hammurabi in his 40th year of kingdom. The Code has 282 Laws; nevertheless some articles can be divided into other articles.

The Code takes into consideration twelve kind of crimes: crimes of witchcraft, crimes in front a judge, crimes against property, crimes related to family, damage to physical integrity of people, crimes related with professions and trade, crimes related to an ox, men killed by an ox, farm workers, shepherds, farm work salaries, slaves.

If we consider that we are talking of 1,754 BC the Code is very advanced in front to others of hundreds of year after.

* * *

Assyria

Other important empire in this area was Assyria, located in the North of Mesopotamia favored by the Tigris, one of the two rivers that permitted to flourish several civilizations in Mesopotamia. Assyria has two important cities: Assur and Ninive. Its beginnings can be established around the middle of the third millennium BC lasting until the beginning of the sixth century BC. The name of the empire comes from the importance of its capital Assur.

The history of Assyria is united to other civilizations such as the Sumerian, Akkadian and Babylonian, sometimes as ruler and others, as ruled.

It cannot be said that Assyria was an empire throughout its existence, as most of the other civilizations in the area was successively invaded or ruled by other people and it had its preponderancy when was ruled by the adequate king as it happened with Esarhaddon who in 671 AC invaded Egypt and put in the power an Egyptian princes to represent him.

With Ashurbanipal, during 42 years as from the year 669 BC, the empire expanded to all the territories at the North, East and South of the East end of Mediterranean Sea, to say it briefly because the list of countries conquered is too large.

In the peak of hegemony of the Empire, two disturbing elements that are always present in extended dominations arose: first, the difficulty of controlling the territories conquered and second, lack of the motor of the advances: the king! After the death of Ashurbanipal, to the periphery problems in several places, Assyria suffered internal disturbances that made the empire to begin to weaken, not only attempting to control the internal problems but also in wars with different contender kings.

The external territories began also to liberate themselves of the Assyrian dominium at the time that the periphery colonies began to be attacked and sacked by other people, especially by the Scythians, with almost a total impunity.

Soon what it was Assyria, went from domination to domination: Medes, Seleucid, Achaemenid, Parthian, Romans and Sasanians until the Assyrian culture almost disappeared crushed by the different invaders.

Persian Empire

To finish with this geographic area we have to speak of the Persian Empire, formed by successive dynasties of which we will mention only those appeared before our era: The Achaemenid Empire (550/330 BC); Seleucid Empire (312/63 BC) and Parthian (or Arsacid) Empire (247 BC/224 AC).

The Persian Empire was located in the territory of Iran and had its origin in 550 BC with Cyrus the Great who conquered Babylon, Media and Lidia.

This first Persian Empire or Achaemenid Empire under the direction of Cyrus the Great became the largest empire in the world until that moment.

Its political and social organization was headed by Cyrus "King of Kings" and under him a large number of governors named Satraps that framed a successful central administration including a good system of communications and postal service, its own language that was used in all territories and the system of defense to preserve the interior life and security against external raids.

The **Achaemenid Empire** reached a population of around 50 million people and to have an idea of the importance of the Empire, just think that Germany, France, Italy, Spain and Portugal together have an approximated extension of less than two millions square kilometers against the five million square kilometers that the Achaemanid Empire reached at that time.

Of course the empire suffered the internal disorders common in large empires, but its strength permitted continuity even after the conquests of Alexander the Great.

The **Seleucid Empire** existed from 312 BC to 63 BC; his founder was Seleucus I who received Babylon from the division of the Macedonian empire after the death of Alexander the Great, territory that he expanded to all Mesopotamia, Persia, Afghanistan and other neighboring territories.

The Seleucid Empire was characterized for its Hellenistic tendency; the Greek influence in the dominant classes was notorious as the abundant and constant immigration from Greeks to most cities.

The beginning of the fall was caused by the war encounters with the Roman legions that frustrated also the possibility to defeat Egypt in the hands now of the Ptolemaic due to the Rome requirements.

Besides, in the second Century BC the Parthians under the Command of Mithritades I, conquered the East part of the empire.

The empire began to increase power again with Antiochus III, son of Seleucus II, who began to rule in 223 BC. Antiochus wanted to demonstrate himself that he was the best after Seleucus I, and began an escalade of conquests crossing the Caucasus and arriving to India where he got an important quantity of elephants to be used in war.

At his return to the West in 205 BC, Seleucus knew about the death of Ptolemy IV and decided to use the opportunity to get in agreement with Philip V of Macedon to invade and divide between them the territories that Ptolemy had outside Egypt, with which Antiochus restored the old prestige of the Empire.

Antiochus died in 187 BC and the Seleucid Empire was soon weakened by the powerful influence of Rome. Antiochus' son Seleucus IV was assassinated by Heliodorus his own minister. Due to the preponderancy of its ruler Arsaces I, the Seleucid Empire was also known as **Arsacid Empire.**

The hegemony of the Seleucid Empire was substituted by the **Parthian Empire** (247 BC-224 AD).

Parthia a satrapy of the Seleucid Empire had rebelled against the empire and soon Mithridates I of Parthia conquered the Seleucid territories of Mesopotamia and Media continuing its expansion in that area becoming an important center of commerce due to its favored location above the Silk Road that came from the China Han Empire to the Roman Empire.

The culture of the Parthian Empire was influenced by the diversity of its territory though the Hellenistic prevailed until later, the Persian influence took relevance. The satrapies in the style of the Achaemenid Empire were changed in many cases by vassal's kingdoms and those satrapies that survived were because their faraway location and their reduced power.

The main enemy of Parthians was Roma, not only by the rivalry on the kingdom of Armenia but also in the East where wars favored alternatively both parts; it deserves to be mentioned the battle of Carrhae (53 BC), the Roman legions led by Crassus suffered one of the worse defeats in the Rome history, the parthians commanded by Surena killed

20,000 Romans, captured 10,000 and Crassus was killed though by a misunderstanding.

The victory of Surena was highly celebrated; nevertheless Orodes II afraid of the ambition of Surena ordered his execution short time after.

With victories and defeats on both sides, war continued until around 224 AC when the Arsacid Empire was substituted by the Sassanid Empire.

Carthaginian Empire

Other empire that achieved hegemony before the first century of our era especially in North Africa and Western Mediterranean was the Carthaginian Empire. The city of Carthage was founded originally in the ninth Century BC by the Phoenicians, a civilization of traders and sailors that established colonies all over the Mediterranean Sea with two great political Centers: Tyre and Sidon in the East of Mediterranean Sea.

When king Belus II of Tyre died, he left his kingdom to his two sons Pygmalion and Dido. Pygmalion was a bad man who wanted the entire kingdom for himself; his sister Dido married his uncle Acerbas, a very rich man and the high priest of Melgart. Pygmalion jealous of the power of Acerbas assassinated him in the temple and Dido afraid of her brother, abandoned Tyre with all her faithful Tyrius followers; and on 840 BC created the city of Carthage located in North Africa under the old Sardinia, in the actual Tunisia. Seven years later Carthage was a flourishing city.

The foundation of Carthage lies between history and legend and there are several versions completely different. Carthage was under the influence of Tyre and so was until the middle of the seven Century BC when it achieved its independence.

About the foundation of Carthage there is a curious anecdote that tells that Dido arrived to the location where Carthage would be built and she asked King Jarbas to sell her an extension of land to build the city. Jarbas accepted to sell but only the land that could be inside the skin of a bull. Dido made his people cut the bull's skin in very thin strips achieving a large extension of land, where Carthage was established. The legend tells that Jarbas impressed by the beauty and intelligence of Dido wanted to marry her menacing her that if she did not accept he would declare war. Dido ordered to prepare a pyre to a sacrifice and put herself in it.

And well known is the passage from the Aeneid of Virgil, between fantasy and reality, that tells how Aeneas after left Troy arrived to Carthage where Dido (Queen Elissa for the Greeks) granted him and his men asylum but soon she fell in love with him wishing that he remained to reign with her, but Aeneas did not accept because he said that his mission was to found Rome and then abandoned Carthage.

According to Virgil, Elissa was so distraught that ordered lift a pyre to put in fire, on which she put herself and deprived of her life with Aeneas' own sword. Before dying she predicted an eternal hostility between Rome and Carthage as so it was.

During almost all its existence Carthage was in war with the Greeks colonies in Sicily. It needed to fight also with the Berbers, the original occupants of the place where Carthage was located.

The other enemy was Rome with whom it fought the three Punic wars and as if the curse of the Queen Elissa were working, the hostility was always permanent. On Rome's side it deserves to be remembered the famous phrase so many times repeated by Cato the Elder: "Cartago delenda est" (Carthage must be destroyed).

After Dido, Carthage had two great generals Amilcar Barca and Anibal.

After the third Punic War, Carthage was destroyed and totally remodeled by Rome which also conquered several other Phoenicians colonies of the north of Africa.

Roman Empire

There is a civilization that in spite of any failures that could have had, it was an example for future civilizations by the scope of its organization and the perfection of its legal institutions that continue being used nowadays. This was the Roman Empire that arrived as an outcome to the long career of the Roman Republic and the continuous internal and external struggles that led Rome to extend its domination to all Southern Europe, North of Africa and parts of Asia. Now it was governed by Emperors; and at that time, those who were Roman citizens were proud of it.

Rome was the largest city in the world with an oriental capital in Byzantium, later named Constantinople in honor to Constantine. It reached to the top of its power through more than 500 years of Republic full of internal and external wars. After their stunning victories that led Rome to a political apogee, Julius Cesar was appointed perpetual Dictator, but was assassinated in 44 BC and more wars and intrigues of any kind followed until the Roman Senate granted to Octavian (27 BC -14 AC), the adopted son of Julius Cesar the title of Augustus and Emperor of Rome ending thus the Republican Period of Rome and beginning an unprecedented period of peace of almost 200 years what was named the *Pax Romana.*

New disorders of any kind clouded the life in the Empire. Constantine (306-337 AC) united the Empire again and shifted the capital to Byzantium that in honor to him, as it was said, was renamed Constantinople.

It was Theodosius I the Great the last emperor who ruled over the West and East sides of the empire, after his dead in 395 AC, the western part of the Empire began to disintegrate surviving until 476 AC when after multiple invasions Romulus Augustulus (Romulus Augustus in Latin) had to accept to assign the government of Rome to Odoacer the head of some Germanic invaders.

Constantinople as Capital of the Eastern Roman Empire also named Byzantine Empire, passed according to the capacity of its various rulers by different situations, it was relevant and deserve to be mentioned the time of Justinian I (527-565) even though his time had to suffer a pandemic that was named the Plague of Justinian, a kind of bubonic plague that affected the **Eastern Roman Empire (Byzantine Empire)**, killed between 25 and 50 million people and it seems that the original focus of infection was China.

The Byzantine Empire was loosing power and territory besieged by constants wars and attacks of the growing Islamic power and even of the Crusades originated in the West, the members of the Fourth Crusade sacked Constantinople that in spite of that and many other adverse situations lasted until 1453 during the time of Constantine XI (1449-1453) when on May 29, 1453 Mehmed the Conqueror took Constantinople.

Egypt

Although it was not properly an empire according to our definition, because its borders in spite of some territories added, were reasonably linked to the limits of its territory, it was however the one that left for posterity majestic remains only comparable to those of the Roman Empire. This was Egypt, the land of the pharaohs.

We find in Egypt several periods of existence: A first and dark period before the Old Kingdom that lasted more than 400 years and we can name Early Period in contraposition with the Late Period, after the third Intermediate Period that in fact was a continuation of it, the Old Kingdom (2686-2181 BC), First Intermediate Period (2181-2055 BC), Middle Kingdom (2055-1650 BC), second Intermediate Period (1650-1550 BC), New Kingdom (1550-1069 BC), Third Intermediate Period (1069-664 BC), Late Period (664-332 BC)

The **Early Period** followed the natural process of most civilizations that appeared in the world: establishing centers of population near a water source, in this case the Nile river, the apparition of the first king Narmer or Meni (better known as Menes), is between myth and reality, and the unification of upper and lower Egypt, around the 3100 BC or more possibly through a slow process, marks the beginning of the apparition of what later was Egypt.

In this period the priest Manetho made a list of 30 dynasties of kings or pharaohs from Manes to his time, showing the importance that already in that time had the religious class. It was then also when the capital was established in Memphis for a better control of the agricultural production.

During the five centuries of the **Old Kingdom** It was built part of the most magnificent constructions that we can still see today as the famous Giza pyramids. It was a spleendorous time of crops of great productivity that needed to have available large quantities of people both in plantations and in construction.

A central strong government made possible such a progress but paradoxically their own progress caused the declination of pharaoh's power. Effectively, the control of the country needed to have several governors named nomarchs that were increasing their power ignoring the central control, with abuse on people and giving more attention to their own interest than to the general interest of the country.

This situation was connected with around 50 years of droughts that resulted in bad crops, which caused desperate moments in people and extreme weakness in the power of Pharaoh during the sixth dynasty, and after internal fights and even famine for around the 130 years of the **First Intermediate Period** that ended in 2055, when Nebhepetre Mentuhotep from the South of Upper Egypt defeated the rulers of the Lower Egypt, beginning a new period of welfare that continued until 1650 BC and was named the Middle Kingdom.

Let us see now how political life was in ancient Egypt. The government was in the hands of a central ruler, the pharaoh. The economy was the result of agriculture, with a barter system at the beginning that changed to a monetary one through the contacts with other civilizations, so the first taxes were paid to the government with products from agriculture or mining.

The government maintained the peace in the territory and stored agriculture products to be distributed among population in scarcity moments.

In primitive civilizations the mass of population was ignorant and ignorance is the seed for superstition. Of course it was easy to move people to a blind belief in any of the so many religions created by men that dominate people by fear to the Unknown, especially to the after life.

Egypt was not an exception, the social distribution of importance from top to bottom began with the gods that rule and influenced everything. Here on earth the gods were represented by the Pharaoh, a kind of living God who had the responsibility for the general welfare of the citizens. Under the Pharaoh were the officials of the Government formed by the noble class and the priests, the priests as intermediary with the gods had great power on the population, because they were also supported by the Pharaoh.

Inside the Government structure soldiers and scribes follow, the first one maintains internal peace, protects population against foreign invasions and supervised the lower level of the population as farmers and slaves. The scribes had an administrative function letting constancy of all new rules and decisions.

The last level was the one formed by the population in which we can also find classes, that, from up to down are: Merchants, artisans and farmers.

Agriculture and mining were the economic support of the country.

Finally as existed in almost all ancient countries there were the slaves, usually people captured in war that were used at discretion of noble classes and as workers in the construction of great monuments.

How Egypt was, from a political point of view, is easy to deduct: an authoritarian government supported by a religious structure. Disobey the pharaoh was to disobey God.

The Middle Kingdom

The experience of the Old Kingdom was taken into account in the Middle Kingdom; with a same structure, the sphere of influence and consequently the power of the officials were reduced increasing their number with respect to the Old Kingdom and the payment of taxes of individuals was more controlled, as well as the activity of nomarchs.

The Middle Kingdom had a duration of 400 years after which Egypt went through a new period of crisis, **The Second Intermediate Period** lasted one hundred years, approximately from 1650 BC end of the Middle Kingdom to 1550 BC when the **New Kingdom** began with several political and administrative changes attempting to avoid past problems, some pointing to agriculture and some to military organization.

It is relevant to note the increasing of the priesthood power and the decisions of judges that until then were based in the evidence of each case, were changed now to verdicts made by a god image interpreted by priests, which made injustice and corruption proliferate, situation that lasted and increased during almost 500 years until a new crisis gave place to a **Third Intermediate Period** that extended along 400 years until 664 BC when the **Late Period** began for something more of 300 years of great changes with the conquest of Egypt by Persia and the Roman Empire.

This finish a superficial examination to the great governments existed in Occident and Middle East before our era. For a better analysis comparative of the political structures of Orient and Occident we will do now a final commentary about the Chinese Empire.

* * *

The China Empire

We will overlook the ancient times of China to refer only to the Imperial period before our era, which began in the Third Century BC with the Qin dynasty that lasted scarcely fifteen years, possibly from 221 BC until the 206 BC.

Anyway, remains have been found from the end of the third millennium in a civilization that was born, as many others, at a river's shore, remember Mesopotamia with the Tigris and Euphrates and Egypt with the Nile. In China the rivers that saw their civilization to grow up were the Yellow River and the Yangtze River.

Also written texts were found from the time of the Shang Dynasty that began 16 Centuries BC. The "Bamboo Annals" are interesting; though they are from the Third Century BC, inform us how the Xia Dynasty was, that began at the end of the third millennium BC.

Qin Dynasty

The Qin Dynasty with its capital in Xianyang, was founded on 221 BC by Qin Shi Huang who achieved the unification of China. What draws the attention in the government of Qin Shi Huang are the so many achievements accomplished in only 15 years and the great influence of his contributions that have reached up to our time.

Qin Shi Huang was the first and last Qin Emperor, having subdued many of the Han dominium and established a central government based in the law strictly controlled by him the emperor, nevertheless while his policy of government worked in the battle field, the hard repression against his opponents created an internal discomfort, that, in part of the population, materialized itself in frequent disturbances.

However his contributions were notorious, the centralized government put an end to the majority of the small wars with the warlords that had been terrifying the population, and the implementation of a central law gave stability and legal security to the population. A regulation on measurements was established, also the use of currency and dispositions about transport that helped commercial relations, motivated the use of the written language and it also deserves to mention his Terracotta Army and the Great Wall of China.

On the other side, while repressed dissidents, burned out books and punished dissident students, he created and trained an intellectual group of official Scholars with high consideration, that were selected through a strict imperial examination where they had to demonstrate their skill in calligraphy, knowledge of Confucian philosophy and good manners because they were considered as gentlemen.

In my opinion the best achievement of Qin Shi Huang was to have finished with dependence of people to the personal decisions of each governor and substitute it by the general subdue to the existent law.

After the Qin Shi Huang' extraneous death, the capital Xianyang was sacked by his opponents, although his work of unification was not lost and the new China's dynasty continued unified.

The Qin Dynasty was substituted by the <u>Han Dynasty</u> (the Western Han) founded by <u>Liu Bang</u> who was the winner in the civil war that followed the death of the emperor of the Qin Dynasty. The Han Dynasty lasted almost 400 years and consolidated the unification promoted by the Qin Dynasty in a long period of stability and welfare under a central unified and legal administration.

This dynasty regulated by law and order, although interrupted occasionally by political events, lasted to our time. During the Han Dynasty there were great advances in science, culture and art that were impossible in those previous situations of instability before the unification.

It deserves to be mentioned in *"the Nine Chapters on the Mathematical Art"* the *"chapter Eight Rectangular Arrays"* the row reduction, mathematical algorithm to solve linear equations that is known now as

Gaussian elimination by his author Carl Friedrich Gauss (1777-1855) and that was already known in China in the Han Dynasty, that is to say, around 1500 years before Gauss.

As well as the law ruled civil life, moral life was conditioned by Confucianism, a philosophy that acted as a true religion without the mental pressure, mercantilism or ostentation of western religions. Following the advice of the Confucianism rules, the Chinese community remained well organized and stable guided by right coexistence advising.

China, during the Han Dynasty had to deal with the military pressure of the Xiongnu Empire in the North of the Great Wall, while began to establish commerce with the west that connected them with the Roman Empire: the *Silk Road.*

Ending the Second Century the Han dynasty developed with the Emperor Wu an imperialist activity necessary to avoid invasions and internal problems that came also in establishing relations with other neighboring kingdoms.

Xin Dynasty

Disappeared Wu, several incapable and inefficient emperors took China to a decline. Abuses on the property of land, expensive military campaigns and a bad influence of the important families that modified political decisions result in the temporal end of the Dynasty that was usurped in the 9 AD by Wang Mang who is said to have a Heaven inspiration to finish the Han Dynasty to substitute it by the "Xin (new) Dynasty",

Wang Mang began a kind of Agrarian reform that was opposed by the owners of the land, lead to chaos and even to the loss of some not well attended peripherals territories of the country.

This Xin Dinasty ended in the death of Wang Mang who was killed in his Palace of Weiyang on 23 AD in a peasant's revolt.

Even though we have limited the brief study of the old empires to those existent before our era, I would like to make a brief overview of the further evolution of China.

Ended the ephemeral Xin Dynasty, the owners of the land, and merchants who suffered the reforms of Wang Mang supported the Emperor Guangwu to reinstate the Han

Dynasty, this time at Luoyang, east of Xi'an beginning in this way the **Eastern Han Dynasty**. An efficient administration with the best of former times put an end to the permanent menace of the Xiongnu Empire and the territory was expanded to the West. Confucianism although continued to our days suffered in that time the strong rivalry of Buddhism. The Silk Road was also reinstated and the contacts with the West were strengthened with Roman ambassadors sent to China. As the Western one, the Eastern Han dynasty was a revival of splendor in science and culture, among others it deserves to mention, by its importance, the invention of paper manufacturing.

It seems that unavoidably the exercise of power produces a wear that puts and end to any government and so it happened also with the Han Dynasty in the Second Century with apparition of the individualism represented by several warlords that made disappear the efficient centralization of the Qin and Han dynasties, movements that got some stabilization under the government of the Three Kingdoms that lasted around 60 years (220-280 AD) during which the power was in the hand of the great families.

Along the history of the world many dynasties and other governments ruled the destiny of

China: Jin, Sui, Tang, Liao, Song, Yuan, Ming are most of them until finally on 1644 the Qing Dynasty was installed that lasted until 1912 when the Republic of China was established. During that long period of more than 1600 years China went through all kind of experiences and suffered invasions and colonialism due the inferiority of its weapons in comparison with the ones of the west.

In 1899, near the end of the Qing dynasty a rebellion exploded promoted by the Yihetuan Movement, known as the Boxer Rebellion that was against foreigners, Christians and colonialism and was a natural consequence of the continuous abuses suffered from the European invaders and Christian missionaries that were trying to reinstate in China in the nineteenth century what they had done in America three hundred years before.

As a continuation and as a result of the weakness of the country the idea of eliminating the Qing Dynasty began to spread and substitute it by a Republic, idea promoted by the revolutionary Sun Yat-sen that found great support in military officers and students and materialized in the revolt of October 1911 and concluded with the installation in Nanjing of the Provisional Government of the Republic of China on March 12, 1912.

And now to end our brief comment about the Imperial China and its final outcome in our time that began with the installation on 1912 of the Republic of China and continued with the Chinese Civil War of 1949 relocating the government to Taipei and the installation of the Communist Party of China proclaimed by Mao Zedong on October 1st, 1949 that is out of our scope of study. We can add that after the death of Mao Zedong a new chapter in the history of China began to open under the direction of Deng Xiaoping, with that seems China is destined to play an important role in the future of the World.

Bibliography

Aubry O. "La Révolution Française" Spanish version of Jordana de Pozas R.M. Luis de Caralt, Barcelona

Ballester R. El Imperio Romano

Birnbaum Immanuel Kleine Geschichte der Sowjetunion. Spanish version of Nelida Mendilaharzu

Bloch L. "Roma Antigua" Ed. Andina, Buenos Aires.

Ceram C.W. "El misterio de los Hititas" translation from German of Gascón J. Ed. Destino, Barcelona

Druon Maurice "Alexandre La Grand" Translation of Jesús López Pacheco, Ed. Cid. España

FREUND, J. "La esencia de lo político" Ed. Nacional, Madrid.

Jiménez de Parga y Cabrera M. "Los regimenes políticos contemporáneos" Ed. Tecnos, Madrid

Kaster, Heinrich L. Kleine Geschichte des Orients. Spanish version of J.J. Thomas

Marx, Carlos "El Capital" Ed. E.D.A.F. Madrid 1967

Montanelli I. Storia di Roma. 1959

Nelson Rowe D. "Modern China a Brief History" Ed. D. Van Nostrand Co, Inc. New Jersey

Oman, Sir Charles "Seven Roman Statesmen" Ed. Edward Arnold, Londres. Versión en español "Siete Estadistas Romanos" Ed. Pegaso. Madrid.

Rojas C. "Napoleón" Gasso Hnos. Barcelona

Roux, G. "Ancient Iraq" Ed. Penguin.

Tarle E. "Napoléon" Version espanola de Delia Ingenieros. Ed. Futuro, Buenos Aires

Van Loon H.W. "Historia de la Humanidad" Ed. Ercilla. Santiago de Chile

Van PARIJS, Ph. "¿Qué es una sociedad justa? Ed. Ariel. Barcelona.

Other Publications of this author:

English:

A Possible Origin (Historic Fiction) Novel
Basic Knowledge (Self knowledge)
Nick (Political Dissertations)
Spirit and Soul (Spiritualism)
The Myth of Politics (Political Dissertations)
Theatre (Three short plays)
Three widows (Criminal Investigation) Novel

Spanish:

Alma y Espíritu (Espiritualismo)
Conocimiento Básico (Auto conocimiento)
El Mito de la Política (Disertaciones políticas)
La Inquietud de Nick (Disertaciones políticas)
Teatro (Tres obras cortas)
Tres Viudas (Investigación criminal) Novela
Un Posible Origen (Ficción histórica) Novela
Viento del Alma (Poemas)

(Available all over the World in Amazon)